☑ **W9-AGM-360**

Communication Skills

TRAINING

Includes CD-ROM with
Ready-to-Use Microsoft
PowerPoint™ Presentations

Exercises, Handouts, Assessments, and Tools
to Help You:
- ✔ Train Individuals, Teams, or Work Groups
  to Communicate More Effectively
- ✔ Quickly Develop Presentation, Listening,
  Negotiation, and Conflict Resolution Skills
- ✔ Become a More Effective and Efficient Facilitator
- ✔ Ensure Training Is on Target and Gets Results

 **ASTD Press**

**Maureen Orey
Jenni Prisk**

ASTD Press is an internationally renowned source of insightful and practical information on workplace learning and performance topics, including training basics, evaluation and return-on-investment (ROI), instructional systems development (ISD), e-learning, leadership, and career development.

Ordering Information: Books published by ASTD Press can be purchased by visiting our Website at store.astd.org or by calling 800.628.2783 or 703.683.8100.

Library of Congress Catalog Card Number: 2004109347

ISBN: 978-1-56286-371-5

Acquisitions and Development Editor: Mark Morrow

Copyeditor: Christine Cotting, UpperCase Publication Services, Ltd.

Interior Design and Production: UpperCase Publication Services, Ltd.

Cover Design: Ana Ilieva

Cover Illustration: Todd Davidson

Printed by Victor Graphics, Inc. Baltimore, Md.
www. victorgraphics.com

The ASTD Trainer's WorkShop Series is designed to be a practical, hands-on road map to help you quickly develop training in key business areas. Each book in the series offers all the exercises, handouts, assessments, structured experiences, and ready-to-use presentations needed to develop effective training sessions. In addition to easy-to-use icons, each book in the series includes a companion CD-ROM with PowerPoint™ presentations and electronic copies of all supporting material featured in the book.

The books in the Trainer's Workshop Seriies include:

- *Coaching Training*
  Chris W. Chen

- *Communication Skills Training*
  Maureen Orey and Jenni Prisk

- *Customer Service Training*
  Maxine Kamin

- *Diversity Training*
  Cris Wildermuth with Susan Gray

- *Innovation Training*
  Ruth Ann Hattori and Joyce Wycoff

- *Leadership Training*
  Lou Russell

- *Leading Change Training*
  Jeffrey Russell and Linda Russell

- *New Employee Orientation Training*
  Karen Lawson

- *New Supervisor Training*
  John E. Jones and Chris W. Chen

- *Project Management Training*
  Bill Shackelford

- *Sales Training*
  Jim Mikula

- *Strategic Planning Training*
  Jeffrey Russell and Linda Russell

- *Teamwork Training*
  Sharon Boller

Contents

Preface   ix

Chapter 1   *INTRODUCTION: HOW TO USE THIS BOOK*   *1*
EFFECTIVELY

The Importance of Self-Preparation for the Facilitator   1
Understanding the Differences in Communication Styles   2
How to Use This Workbook   3
What's on the CD?   5
Icons   5
What to Do Next   6

Chapter 2   *IDENTIFYING COMMUNICATION NEEDS*   *7*
WITHIN AN ORGANIZATION

Understanding the Impact of Diversity on an Organization   7
How Communication Can Affect Organizational Dynamics   8
Workplace Relationships   9
Surveying Participants and Assessing Needs   12
What to Do Next   12

Chapter 3   *DESIGNING YOUR COMMUNICATION SKILLS*   *15*
WORKSHOP

Purpose and Goals of Your Training Program   15
Basic Instructional Design   16
Preparing the Environment for Learning   21
Training Materials   21
What to Do Next   22

Chapter 4   *FACILITATING YOUR COMMUNICATION SKILLS*   *23*
WORKSHOP

Preparations for the Workshop   23
Facilitator Materials   24

Participant Materials   25

Facilitator Responsibilities   28

Welcome and Introduction   29

Responding to Questions   30

Why Things Go Bad   32

What to Do Next   33

**Chapter 5 EVALUATING YOUR COMMUNICATION SKILLS   35
WORKSHOP**

Why Evaluate Your Program?   35

What to Evaluate and How to Do It   35

When to Evaluate Your Program   39

Participants' Follow-Up Evaluation   40

What to Do Next   42

**Chapter 6 ONE-HOUR SESSION: COMMUNICATIONS   43
OVERVIEW**

Objectives of the One-Hour Session   43

Materials   44

Using the CD   44

Sample Agenda   44

What to Do Next   47

Chapter 7 HALF-DAY COMMUNICATION SKILLS WORKSHOP   51

Objectives of the Half-Day Session   51

Materials   52

Using the CD   53

Sample Agenda   53

What to Do Next   61

Chapter 8 FULL-DAY COMMUNICATION SKILLS WORKSHOP   67

Objectives of the Full-Day Session   68

Materials   68

Using the CD   70

Preparation   70

Sample Agenda   70

What to Do Next   81

Chapter 9   ***TWO-DAY COMMUNICATION SKILLS WORKSHOP***   **89**

Objectives of the Two-Day Session   92
Materials   92
Using the CD   94
Sample Agenda   94
What to Do Next   103

Chapter 10   ***LEARNING ACTIVITIES***   **111**

Learning Activity 10–1: Icebreaker: Getting to Know You   112
Learning Activity 10–2: Understanding Yourself   114
Learning Activity 10–3: Icebreaker: Life Is Just a Bowl of   117
   Candies
Learning Activity 10–4: The Listening Stick   118
Learning Activity 10–5: Active Listening Role Play   120
Learning Activity 10–6: Visual Listening   122
Learning Activity 10–7: One on One   124
Learning Activity 10–8: Icebreaker: Class Reunion   125
Learning Activity 10–9: Interpersonal Skills   126
Learning Activity 10–10: I Want It!   127
Learning Activity 10–11: Ten Questions About Conflict   129
Learning Activity 10–12: Persuasion   130
Learning Activity 10–13: Persuasion Strategy   132
Learning Activity 10–14: Negotiation Outcomes   134
Learning Activity 10–15: Feedback Experience   135
Learning Activity 10–16: Johari Window   138
Learning Activity 10–17: Assertiveness—Making Your Case   141
Learning Activity 10–18: Vocal Exercises   143
Learning Activity 10–19: Storytelling   145
Learning Activity 10–20: Analogies   147

Chapter 11   ***ASSESSMENTS***   **149**

Assessment 11–1: Client Survey and Needs Analysis   151
Assessment 11–2: Participant Survey and Needs Analysis   154
Assessment 11–3: Supervisor's Evaluation of Employee   156
   Participant
Assessment 11–4: Listening Skills   157
Assessment 11–5: Interpersonal Skills   158

Assessment 11–6: Negotiation Skills and Readiness   159

Assessment 11–7: Course and Facilitator Evaluation   160

Assessment 11–8: Learning Comprehension Level   161

Assessment 11–9: Skills Mastery   162

Assessment 11–10: Skills Application   163

Chapter 12 TOOLS   **165**

Tool 12–1: Frequently Used Action Verbs   166

Tool 12–2: Journal Pages   167

Tool 12–3: Tips for Understanding Body Language   169

Tool 12–4: One on One   170

Tool 12–5: Maslow's Hierarchy of Needs   171

Tool 12–6: Nonconfrontational Language—Using "I" Rather Than "You"   172

Tool 12–7: Skills for Interpersonal Success   173

Tool 12–8: Pointers for Developing Interpersonal Skills and the Benefits of Doing So   174

Tool 12–9: Five Steps to Resolving Conflict   175

Tool 12–10: Persuasion Guidelines   176

Tool 12–11: Negotiation Strategies   177

Tool 12–12: Simple Guidelines for Giving Feedback   178

Tool 12–13: Conflict in Team Meetings   179

Tool 12–14: Fun Phrases and Tongue Twisters   180

Tool 12–15: Delivery Skills for Effective Presentations   181

Tool 12–16: What Influences an Audience   183

Tool 12–17: Steps for Developing a Three-Point Presentation   184

Tool 12–18: All About Storytelling   185

Tool 12–19: Using Stories and Analogies   186

Tool 12–20: Strategies for Effective Meetings   187

Appendix USING THE COMPACT DISC   **189**

Contents of the CD   189

Computer Requirements   189

Printing From the CD   190

Adapting the PowerPoint Slides   191

Showing the PowerPoint Presentations   191

For Further Reading   193

About the Authors   195

At any given moment around the world, people are communicating. They are using different approaches, different styles, and different languages, but the desired result is the same... to understand and to be understood.

When we embarked on writing this book we felt overwhelmed by the vastness of communication issues. What should we include, and what should we omit? The topic is almost limitless. We knew that for this book to be practical and realistic, we had to call on our own experiences in training, coaching, and facilitating communication, and ask ourselves "what would we want to read?" In fact, Maureen was searching for just such a book when she discovered that a trainer's workshop guide for communication didn't exist. How do you fix that problem? Well, you find a colleague and friend and you write it together.

Many of you are seasoned facilitators who already are using many of these designs and formats for your workshops. We believe that we have offered you some new insights in the learning modules. For those of you who are new to communication facilitation, we know that you can create a comfortable process from the content in this book.

Effective communication is the key to success in our professional and personal lives. The right strategy, carefully chosen words, and respect extended through communication can be the making of a team or an individual. Communication is the very stuff that supports our lives.

We have had a lot of fun and, of course, have done a lot of communicating and eaten a lot of chocolate while writing this book. Maureen is extremely grateful to her three children, Shane, Rachel, and Danielle, for being such great kids and bearing with Mom while she's been preoccupied with the book—I love you. Many thanks to Carl and Jennifer for caring for the children during those long Saturday writing sessions. Also, a huge thank-you to

Vey for his help, support, and encouragement in this process. Thank you to all of my colleagues at ASTD—I've learned a lot from you all.

Jenni especially thanks her husband, Kim, for his patience and support throughout the writing process. She is also grateful to her many clients who have given her inspiration and wisdom. And she is thankful for her mentor, Sam, who constantly opens her mind to possibilities. And without Mark Morrow of ASTD Press this book would never have been published. Thank you, Mark, for your support, advice, and guidance. We will also be forever grateful to our amazing editor, Christine Cotting, who has a magic way with words.

Maureen Orey
Jenni Prisk
October 2004

◆

Introduction: How to Use This Book Effectively

What's in This Chapter?

- ◆ Discussion of the value of effective communication
- ◆ Discussion of the importance of self-preparation for the facilitator
- ◆ Explanation of how to use this book
- ◆ Description of what's in this workbook and on the CD

For thousands of years, humans have used communication to connect, convey ideas, and develop relationships. Communication skills in the workplace today are one of the most important aspects of organizational dynamics. They affect workplace relationships, departmental relations, company culture, and ultimately the financial health of the organization.

Communication can build or destroy any situation. Clear, concise, and effective communication promotes openness, enables projects or processes to move forward, and enhances relationships. Conversely, poor, unclear, or nonspecific communication in an organization leads to dysfunction, low morale, and costly mistakes.

The Importance of Self-Preparation for the Facilitator

When teaching effective communication skills, the facilitator must relay appropriate information to the participants and must use confident communication skills in the process. Essentially, as a facilitator you must model effective communication skills. It is also important to understand the current needs, issues, and skill levels of your audience. In order to understand your client's needs, it is helpful to administer a needs analysis a week or two before the workshop. A needs analysis can be done via email, online, or in a hard-

copy format, and it may gather information such as current needs, issues, and skills (see Assessment 11–1: Client Survey and Needs Analysis). Furthermore, you must research and analyze the participants to determine as much information as possible about their backgrounds, experiences, and expertise (see Assessment 11–2: Participant Survey and Needs Analysis). A class is quick to discover when the facilitator has not done this preparatory work, and participants may grow bored and resentful.

You have to know the participants' professional roles, educational levels, and cultural backgrounds. This knowledge will help you understand the participants' status, learning capabilities, and language skills. This information can be acquired from the needs analysis, a participant's supervisor, or the organization's human resources department (see Assessment 11–3: Supervisor's Evaluation of Employee Participant). In order for the information about the participant to be focused appropriately for the workshop, consider asking the following questions :

- In what professional situations is the employee required to exhibit clear and concise communication?

- In what areas does the employee experience the greatest challenges in communication?

- What are the employee's communication strengths?

- Which skills would you recommend that this employee learn in a communications workshop?

- What results do you expect for this employee following the communications workshop?

Such knowledge is not foolproof, however, so you should be aware of the supervisor's responses and reactions before the workshop begins. As mentioned previously, it is wise to survey the participants who will reveal useful information about their learning requirements.

Understanding the Differences in Communication Styles

It is important to take into account the many different communication, cultural, and personality styles that will be represented in your training sessions, both in planning your content and in facilitating the communication skills workshops.

Here is an overview of some key personality traits you may encounter:

- **Aggressive:** Wants control; bullies or intimidates others

- **Passive:** "Yes" person; rarely speaks or shares his or her opinion

- **Manipulative:** Works from her or his own agenda

- **Direct:** Will tell you the truth, no matter what.

The variation of personality and communication styles is so vast that we could write another book about it. Suffice it to say that the above traits are frequently mixed and matched to create many more challenging types, such as passive/aggressive and direct/manipulative. As a facilitator, you must be prepared to handle the many challenges that will occur with the pooling of styles, cultures, and personalities.

How to Use This Workbook

Whether you are an experienced trainer or a novice instructor, you will find this workbook a useful resource for developing and facilitating a communication skills workshops. By understanding the basic concepts about effective communication skills and then reviewing the sample training program designs and materials, you will be able to customize the program design for your specific audiences.

The training materials in the book and on the accompanying CD-ROM include the following:

- Tools and strategies for identifying existing communication skills and needs (chapter 2).

- Guidelines for designing communication skills workshops (chapter 3).

- Materials and instructions for facilitating your training sessions (chapter 4).

- Strategies and tools for evaluating the learning (chapter 5).

- Training workshop sample agendas that incorporate a range of training activities. The agendas can be used "as is" or modified to suit your organization, its challenges, and your own teaching style (chapters 6 through 9).

- Learning activities and the assessments and tools designed to support and enhance them (chapters 10 through 12).

◆ Microsoft PowerPoint presentations you can use to focus the attention of workshop participants on the content of the program. Thumbnail versions of all of the slides appear at the end of the chapters in which they are used. The CD also contains black-and-white versions of the slides that can be printed on paper and used as handouts or printed on film and used as overhead masters.

Be sure to prepare the handouts for your training sessions in advance. All of them are included on the CD. You may want to create a notebook for each participant that contains all of the assessments, tools, and slides so they have material to take away after the workshop and refer to on the job.

Here are suggestions for using this book effectively:

◆ **Skim the book.** Quickly read through the entire contents of this workbook. Review the "What's in This Chapter?" lists at the beginning of each chapter. Get a good feel for the layout and structure of what's included in the book.

◆ **Understand the mechanics of effective communication.** Do some research on the topic of communication. Chapter 2 provides important insights about the role of communication in organizations, and chapter 4 provides you with the background information you need to teach each of the different versions of the program. Additionally, the learning activities in chapter 10 provide the opportunities for active learning on a deeper level. The For Further Reading section at the back of the book suggests a number of excellent books on communication topics so that you can explore them in greater depth in preparing for your workshop.

◆ **Assess the existing communication styles within the organization.** It is helpful to understand the current issues regarding the culture and style of communication in the organization. Communication skills affect each person in every part of his or her life, so personal issues will often surface in a workshop. It is crucial to keep the focus on workplace issues and on ways to improve communication on the job. See chapter 11 for sample assessments.

◆ **Review the methods for high-quality training design and for creating a positive learning environment.** In chapter 3 you will review approaches and strategies for identifying the purpose and goals of your program, how to incorporate different learning styles, how to select the workshop content, and how to set the atmosphere for learning. Even if you are an experienced trainer, you will find that a review of this chapter will reinforce what you are already doing—and may add to your toolkit for effective instructional design.

♦ **Explore the sample training program agendas.** Chapters 6 through 9 provide a variety of workshop format options that you can draw on as you design a program to fit your audience. From a one-hour session to a multiday series, you will see a number of training program designs that you can use as is or customize to suit your needs.

♦ **Design your training program.** With your target audience defined and an awareness of the learning activities contained in this workbook, select one of the programs presented here or create your own training sessions.

What's on the CD?

All of the assessments, tools, training instruments, and PowerPoint slides used in this workbook are included on the accompanying CD. Follow the instructions in the appendix, "Using the Compact Disc," at the back of the workbook or read "How to Use This CD.doc" on the CD.

Icons

For easy reference, icons are included in the margins throughout this workbook to help you quickly locate key elements in training design and instruction. Here are the icons and what they represent:

Assessment: Appears when an agenda or learning activity includes an assessment.

CD: Indicates materials included on the CD accompanying this workbook.

Clock: Indicates suggested timeframes for an activity.

Discussion Question: Points out questions to use in exploring significant aspects of the training and debriefing an activity.

Key Point: Alerts you to key points that you should emphasize to the participants or that are particularly salient for you as the facilitator.

Learning Activity: Indicates a structured exercise for use in a training session.

PowerPoint Slide: Indicates PowerPoint presentations and slides that you can use individually.

Tool: Identifies an item that offers information participants will find useful in the training session and on the job.

Training Instrument: Indicates interactive training activities for participant use.

What to Do Next: Denotes recommendations for what to do after completing a particular section of the workbook.

What to Do Next

- ♦ Study the contents of this workbook to learn for yourself what resources it contains.

- ♦ Review the contents of the CD and open a few of the items on it to be sure you know how to access them.

- ♦ Prepare yourself by becoming aware of your own communication style.

♦♦♦

In chapter 2 you will discover the impact that cultural diversity has on an organization and how it shapes the professional environment. In addition, we'll explore organizational dynamics to discover how effective communication influences workplace relationships throughout the entire organization.

◆

Chapter 2

Identifying Communication Needs Within an Organization

What's in This Chapter?

- ◆ Discussion of the impact of diversity on an organization
- ◆ Description of the interplay of communication and organizational dynamics
- ◆ Examination of workplace relationships
- ◆ Discussion of employee surveys and needs assessments

Understanding the Impact of Diversity on an Organization

There are many different styles and cultures in the workplace today. They are not only the products of various races and ethnic backgrounds, but also the products of family dynamics, life experience, and inevitable personal biases. We all bring our own perspective on life to every situation we encounter. Our perspective is a filter through which we view life, and our biases are the dust particles that contaminate the filter. It is essential that you as the facilitator be aware of the dust on your own filter. Our filters need to be inspected and cleaned regularly to make sure that they are not dusty and do not obscure the view.

The role that diversity plays in organizations today is viewed from both a positive and a negative perspective. Viewed positively, diversity enriches an organization, fosters creativity, enables more effective customer service, and creates a more balanced workplace. Viewed negatively, diversity can create barriers to communication; challenge existing corporate values and beliefs; and magnify the differences among those in the workplace, thereby causing intolerance and unrest. This of course is a generalization about the role of diversity in an organization because volumes have been written about this topic.

How Communication Can Affect Organizational Dynamics

As was mentioned in chapter 1, poor communication can contribute to ineffective working relationships, low morale, costly mistakes, reduced job performance, and even malicious withholding of critical information within an organization. Ultimately a commitment must be made to establish an environment of openness and honesty. If there have been many years of poor communication and mistrust, it is likely that it will take some time to rebuild the trust and willingness to be open and honest. Consider your organizational culture along the following lines:

1. Does the organization encourage and reward open and honest communication? (If the answer to this question is "yes," the organization is likely to have a positive and open workplace environment. If the answer is "no," the organization may find it difficult to engage employees and solicit honest feedback.)

2. Does the organization have many closed-door meetings? (If the answer to this question is "yes," the organizational culture may be one of suppression and secrecy, and there will be very little trust within the organization. If the answer is "no," the organizational culture will tend to be more open and flexible, encouraging spontaneous and ongoing communication.)

3. Does the organization withhold information from certain levels of employees? (If the answer to this question is "yes," the organization may have a strict hierarchical structure that creates operational silos and discourages innovation. If the answer is "no," the organization will typically encourage initiative and innovation, thus giving employees access to any information they need to complete their work effectively.)

4. Does the organization make information available to all stakeholders? (If the answer to this question is "yes," the organization will have the culture of a learning organization, empowering employees to be creative, innovative, and involved. If the answer is "no," the organization may have a culture of power and control, and may keep a watchful eye on access to company information.)

In general, responses that reflect a culture of openness and access to information typically identify a positive work environment; responses that reflect a closed and controlling culture in the organization typically identify a negative work environment. To create an effective and successful organization, you must first create a vision for the organization and its culture, and then you must begin to build the appropriate components to enable progress. Improving communication in an organization is only one step toward the goal of a successful and positive organization.

Workplace Relationships

When participants enter a classroom they carry with them the effects of the communication style within their company or organization. Some will come from an environment where the communication is open and comfortable. Others will have evolved in a structured, formal environment. Each participant will be seeking solutions to apply to different situations. Let's break the communication relationships down into separate elements.

INDIVIDUAL COMMUNICATION

The first thing that a parent waits to hear from a child is the sound of the child's voice. We celebrate this event, even when the words are unintelligible. The event indicates a rite of passage into the world of adult interaction. However, not every child grows up in a home where communication is comfortable. A young child absorbs much of the behavior he or she is exposed to before the age of 7, and this pattern of behavior can continue into adulthood.

Therefore, in your class you will have people who communicate better one-to-one than in a group and others who prefer the opposite forum. Some will communicate reticently, some boldly, and some with ease and fluency.

It is your role to identify each learner's natural style early on in the workshop process. Quiet participants generally prefer to listen and observe. Be careful not to regard this as nonengagement and overlook their importance. Respect a person's individuality. Whether a person is introverted or outgoing, he or she deserves deference. Honor a participant's approach and acknowledge his or her input. If you don't do this, you may alienate the student and create a negative atmosphere. When a class sees you demonstrate respect, it is more likely that members will take this approach in their own workplace interactions.

Every group has a person who likes to hold the floor. This person must be acknowledged for his or her input and then reminded of time constraints in the classroom. If the boldness persists, consider giving this person a task or responsibility that consumes energy but makes the person feel important to the process. (This personality type is discussed in chapter 1.)

You can draw out a quiet participant by placing him or her in small work groups where the fear of communication feels less extreme. Partnering this person with someone who communicates openly also supports the development process.

TEAM COMMUNICATION

One of the biggest challenges in team communication is the diversity of individual styles. Completing a personality profile that reveals the range of styles on the team helps members of the team communicate effectively. There are literally hundreds of personality profiling instruments on the market today. This can make the choice of instrument daunting. One test that has been used for 60 years is the *MBTI* or *Myers-Briggs Type Indicator*. A recent report indicates that 89 companies out of the *Fortune* 100 use the *MBTI*. This assessment identifies introverted or extroverted behavior, and whether a person is a thinker or a perceiver, judgmental or intuitive. Another personality test is the *DiSC Personal Profile System.* This instrument uses the four main personality characteristics of domination, influence, steadiness, and conscientiousness. These two tests can be accessed on the Internet and may require licensing before you use them. As a facilitator, occasionally you will group your participants into teams without the benefit of a personality profile. Therefore, it is important that you understand the dynamics of group interaction.

When you assemble a team it is helpful to mix opposing personalities to provide variety and balance in the team exchange. Participants with the same style who group together will not share an enhanced learning experience because they will work within similar parameters.

When a team is formed by participants from different departments within an organization, introduction and icebreaker activities will provide a communication door through which participants can enter comfortably.

DEPARTMENTAL COMMUNICATION

Frequently you will encounter competition among participants from the same department who are maneuvering for superiority or advancement. You have to recognize this behavior and maintain an atmosphere of fairness throughout the training session.

Participants from the same department will often form a solid alliance and challenge other participants who endeavor to team with them. You must recognize this behavior and handle it with care to avoid divisiveness in the workshop. Using random numbering to form groups will help allay this counterproductive pattern.

INTERDEPARTMENTAL COMMUNICATION

Departments in organizations are increasingly forced to collaborate today. Information technology personnel support the entire operation and Human Resources provides guidance and staffing for all departments. Resentment thrives, however, if salaries differ for similar positions among departments, or if promotions are seen to be biased. Again, you must be aware of these challenges and offer an environment in which interdepartmental communication can reach a new level of understanding about the judgments or assessments made in different departments. Mix up participants so that there is a cross-fertilization of information, ideas, and communication styles.

UPWARD VS. DOWNWARD COMMUNICATION

The hierarchy challenge can be one of the toughest in a workshop. The ego of a senior participant can be threatened if his or her weakness in a specific area of communication is highlighted in an activity. Unless a good relationship already exists between the parties, sparks may fly if a subordinate participating in the workshop excels in the senior's weak areas. Conversely, a subordinate may feel stymied in communication when a senior is present because he or she believes that information or ideas expressed could be received in a negative manner and used against the subordinate. Your role is to establish trust and openness and, if necessary, to discuss the situation individually with the appropriate participants.

The purpose of every workshop is to enhance communication so you must set the example and create environmental conditions up front so that a smooth flow of ideas can follow.

INTERNAL VS. EXTERNAL COMMUNICATION

Many organizations require their employees to regard colleagues as clients and to communicate with them with courtesy and respect. This style creates positive synergy throughout the organization and participants from these environments may communicate with openness and directness in the workshop. You must recognize this competency and acknowledge it accordingly.

Participants who work for an organization that positions clients, consultants, and vendors above employees may bring tension and anxiety to the training session. It is important that you recognize this behavior and extend respect and deference to these participants to help them with communication growth. Through the use of effective communication techniques in the workshop, you will provide awareness and understanding of these differing communication styles and thus offer increased understanding for return to the workplace or, even better, new alternatives for improved communication at the participant's workplace.

Surveying Participants and Assessing Needs

Before you design the workshop it is essential that you get feedback from the participants about the topic you will cover in the training so you can develop and customize materials that will respond to the areas of need the employees identify. Handle the surveys in a manner that will ensure confidentiality. If you do so, it is likely that the feedback will be more open and honest.

The survey you design or develop should attempt to capture all types of workplace relationships (individual, teams, departments, and so on). All questions must be free of bias and should not "lead" the respondent to answer in a specific way. There is a sample survey you can use in chapter 11 (Assessment 11–2: Participant Survey and Needs Analysis). In addition, there are many good assessments available commercially. See the resources listed in the For Further Reading section, *Assessments A–Z.*

What to Do Next

- ◆ Consider the diversity in the organization where you'll present a training.

- ◆ Develop or select an employee survey to identify existing communication skills among potential participants.

- ◆ Define the diverse needs of your participants.

- ◆ Identify the various types of communication you will encounter among training participants.

◆ Plan ways to avoid problems inherent in dissimilar communication styles and comfort levels.

◆ ◆ ◆

In chapter 3 you will discover the elements required to design your communication skills workshop. You will learn that it is vital to define the purpose and goals of the workshop from both the participants' and the employers' perspectives. Included also are straightforward ground rules for instructional design and techniques for structuring the learning environment.

Designing Your Communication Skills Workshop

What's in This Chapter?

- Definition of the purpose of your training program in communication skills

- Delineation of the goals of your communication skills workshop

- Discussion of the elements of basic instructional design

- Instructions for preparing the learning environment

Purpose and Goals of Your Training Program

Before you can put together the workshop, you must determine the purpose and goals of the program. Do you simply want to provide your staff with professional development communication skills, or is this program tied to a specific business need or issue within your organization? If the content of the program is linked to a specific need, be sure to incorporate all appropriate topics that will address those issues.

Everyone benefits from a road map. As the facilitator, you must be especially focused on the purpose and goals of your program. Frequently these are defined for you by the organization that you are working for as either an internal employee or an external consultant. It is important that you keep to these parameters and achieve the outcome expected for the workshop and for the participants.

It is equally important for you to understand the individual goals of the participants. You can discover these at the beginning of the first class. Occasionally some goals will fall outside the periphery of the class focus, and these goals should be discussed and documented at the outset. If your class is made up of voluntary participants you may wish to have a private discussion with a participant whose goals are not going to be met by the training to determine whether he or she is enrolled in the appropriate class.

WORKSHOP PURPOSE AND GOALS

The purpose of a communication skills workshop is to provide targeted skills and techniques appropriate to the mission of the organization. The goals of a communication skills workshop are defined by the employing organization, the facilitator, and the participants.

PROGRAM DESIGN GOALS

Your goals in designing a training program in communication skills are

1. to offer a program of communication skills covering a broad spectrum

2. to provide an environment that makes learning accessible

3. to use proven methods of instruction and training

4. to deliver the instruction in ways that meet diverse social and cultural needs

5. to promote discussion and exploration of communication issues

6. to guide participants through communication exercises

7. to monitor and evaluate their progress in learning

8. to determine that students have met their personal and organizational goals at the conclusion of the workshop

9. to supply a road map for personal study after the workshop.

Basic Instructional Design

The design of the workshop needs to incorporate the basic principles of sound instructional design. The ADDDE Principle (Figure 3–1) is a process to use when putting the workshop together:

- ◆ **A**nalyze training needs

- ◆ **D**etermine the learning objectives

- ◆ **D**evelop the training materials

Figure 3-1

The ADDDE Principle

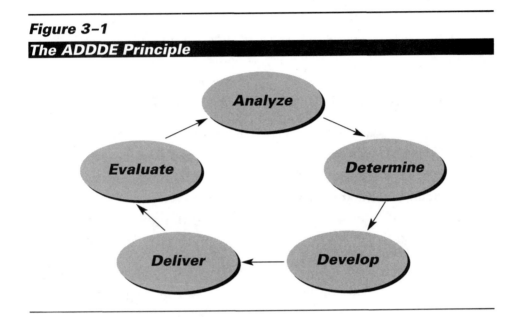

- **D**eliver the training

- **E**valuate and update the training.

We addressed the first of the five facets of the ADDDE Principle in chapter 2. The next two facets are addressed in this chapter. Chapter 4 will explain how to deliver the training, and chapter 5 will explain how to evaluate and update the training.

DETERMINE LEARNING OBJECTIVES

When you have identified the purpose and goals of your program, you must determine which learning objectives will be used to focus the content of the workshop. When writing your objectives, specify concrete accomplishments to be attained in training. Use action verbs, and keep the statements brief and to the point. Here are some examples of learning objectives:

At the end of this workshop, participants will be able to

- *identify their communication styles*

- *understand and use the concepts of active listening*

- *resolve a conflict situation using proactive communication skills*

- *negotiate in diverse situations*

- *give and receive negative and positive feedback.*

Tool 12–1 (in chapter 12 and on the CD) provides a list of frequently used action verbs that will be helpful in writing the learning objectives for your workshops.

STREAMLINING ORAL AND WRITTEN INFORMATION

The Internet has helped us develop our abilities to receive and process information. Therefore, in the classroom it is essential to provide streamlined, efficient communication, both orally and in written training materials. A facilitator who gets to the point quickly while delivering complete details is valued by participants. Although the class may enjoy hearing your personal stories, participants will lose interest if the stories are too frequent and prolonged.

There are several techniques for streamlining oral communication. One technique calls for the facilitator to ask individual participants to read aloud, or deliver from the front of the room, specific learning points from the workshop manual. This provides a change of voice that increases the attentiveness of other participants. Another technique requires the facilitator to write on a board or flipchart the key points of the topic being taught and then to ask individual participants to link the points through small-group discussion or individual narrative.

INCORPORATING DIFFERENT LEARNING STYLES

You must consider the different learning styles of the participants. Simply put, the three learning styles are

- ◆ visual

- ◆ audial

- ◆ kinesthetic.

Visual learners prefer charts, illustrations, images, and physical expression from the trainer. Audial learners like to read and analyze and often shut out visual cues. Kinesthetic learners prefer to be actively and physically involved in the learning through role plays, discussions, and hands-on interactive exercises.

Each learning style has a different focus, values different things, and uses specific language. Here are a few examples:

Visual learners: To reach them, use videos, flipcharts, handouts, icons, symbols, and color.

FOCUS	VALUE	LANGUAGE	SAMPLE COMMENTS
Seeing	Images	See	"Look at it this way."
	Symbols	Picture	"See what I mean?"
	Holistic	Look	"We need a balance."
	strategies and	Vision	"Give me the big picture."
	solutions	Seek	"He can't see the forest for
		Symmetry	the trees."

Audial learners: To reach them, incorporate interactive discussion, dialogue, and lecture.

FOCUS	VALUE	LANGUAGE	SAMPLE COMMENTS
Hearing	Logic	Think	"This sounds good to me."
	Reason	Ideas	"Let me think about it."
	Concepts	Concepts	"Let's hear the numbers."
	Logical strategies	Analyze	"How do you like the idea?"
	and solutions	Hear	"It seems like a logical
		Sound	move."
			"Here are the facts."

Kinesthetic learners: To reach them, include the opportunity to practice what is being learned; use role plays, work samples, and job aids.

FOCUS	VALUE	LANGUAGE	SAMPLE COMMENTS
Touching	Intuition	Feel	"You know what I mean."
	Insight	Touch	"How do you feel about it?"
	Perception	Sense	"Our people won't go for it."
	How people feel	Perceive	"Let's keep in touch."
	about a change	Emotion	"Would you share?"
	or decision	Share	"I'm not comfortable with it."

SELECTING AND DEVELOPING PROGRAM CONTENT

On the basis of the feedback from the client and participant surveys, needs analysis, and from the participants' supervisors (Assessments 11–1, 11–2, and 11–3), you can begin to select the content and topics to include in your work-

shop. The content of your program will depend on specific management requirements, the requirements of the individual participants, or a combination of both. Remember to ensure that basic communication skills, such as listening and responding, are not forgotten in an attempt to customize the workshop to specific requirements. Inherent in the selection of content is the need to target the information to the participants' learning levels. Although content develops from the learning objectives and requirements, it is important to maintain flexibility because communication is a wide-ranging topic. The following is a selection of topics that you may want to include in your communication skills workshops:

- ♦ assertiveness

- ♦ body language

- ♦ confrontational communication

- ♦ cultural differences in communication

- ♦ diverse workplace environments

- ♦ formal vs. informal communication

- ♦ generational communication

- ♦ history and evolution of communication

- ♦ interpersonal communication

- ♦ interviews

- ♦ introduction and discussion of types of communication

- ♦ language and voice

- ♦ leadership communication

- ♦ listening

- ♦ management communication

- ♦ meeting/greeting

- ♦ mentoring

- ♦ negotiation

- ♦ operations communication

- ♦ persuasion

- presentation skills

- public speaking

- self-assessment

- storytelling

- styles of communication

- understanding unique communication styles

- use of language and voice.

Complete communication skills workshops have been developed for you in chapters 6 through 9. The workshops range from a one-hour session to a two-day program that covers most of the topics listed above.

Preparing the Environment for Learning

To maximize your opportunity for success, consider the following aspects when preparing for the workshop:

- maximum number of participants who can be accommodated comfortably and facilitated properly (we suggest no more than 25)

- room temperature

- ventilation

- lighting

- audiovisual needs

- room set-up

- copies of all participant materials for all attendees

- accommodations and materials for people with disabilities

- your arrival time (get there early)

- your adequate preparation.

Training Materials

When you prepare high-quality materials you save classroom time because participants quickly comprehend the information covered in the materials.

The ease with which the students can grasp the message means that time is not wasted on questions to clarify. When you take time to set up learning activities and exercises in advance, workshop time is conserved.

When classroom materials are easily comprehensible, they expedite understanding by the participants. Different typefaces indicate different emphasis. Changes of color on handouts can denote changes of topic. PowerPoint slides should be simple and eye-catching. A picture replaces a thousand words so use illustrations wherever possible. When you use acronyms, supply a glossary for referral. Graphs and charts save lengthy explanations. A simple anecdote or a succinct slogan can explain a complex theory.

Check periodically during a training session to see that your students are catching the information. Occasionally invite participants to summarize a block of learning to ensure that they are on the right track and to let you hear the information you're passing along from an objective point of view.

What to Do Next

- Define the purpose and specific goals of your communication skills workshop.

- Define the learning objectives your content must support.

- Make your content selections on the basis of your needs assessment.

- Decide on the length of your workshop.

- Identify ways in which you can tailor your content to reach all of your students' learning styles.

- Plan your workshop environment to make the most of the time and space you have.

◆ ◆ ◆

In chapter 4 we discuss the preparation needed to facilitate the communications workshop. Included in this discussion are the physical and process requirements, together with the preparation of participants' materials. Also defined are your responsibilities while facilitating the workshop, including appropriate techniques for answering questions.

Facilitating Your Communication Skills Workshop

What's in This Chapter?

- Overview of facilitator's preparations for the workshop

- Instructions for developing participant materials

- Delineation of the facilitator's responsibilities

- Guidelines for responding to questions

Preparations for the Workshop

Preparation is power when it comes to facilitating a successful workshop. The following list of activities will help you prepare:

- Write down all location and workshop details when scheduling the workshop.

- Make travel reservations early (to save money, too).

- Send a contract to the client to confirm details, or if you are an internal facilitator, develop guidelines and a workshop structure in conjunction with appropriate supervisors and managers.

- Specify room and equipment details in writing and then confirm by telephone.

- Define goals and expectations for the workshop.

- Get a list of participants, titles, roles, and responsibilities.

- Send participants a questionnaire that requires them to confirm their goals for the workshop.

◆ Send the client (or the participants, if you are an internal facilitator) an agenda for the workshop, with times for breaks and meals.

◆ Recommend that lunch/dinner be offered in-house, with nutritious food provided.

◆ Make a list of materials that you will need in the room (pads of paper, pens, pencils, markers, flipchart, and so forth).

◆ Design the room layout (for example, U-shape, teaching style, auditorium set-up, half-circle).

◆ Confirm whether you or your internal/external client will prepare copies of the workshop handouts. The workshop handouts should include all tools, training instruments, assessments, and PowerPoint slides.

◆ Find out if participants would like to receive training materials electronically before the session.

◆ Prepare assessments, tools, training instruments, and workshop materials at least one week before the workshop so that you have time to peruse and check them.

Facilitator Materials

When all details for the workshop have been confirmed, it is time to prepare for the actual facilitation of the workshop at the site. You may know the site well because you are providing in-house facilitation. If, however, you are traveling off-site to facilitate, important elements enter the planning. Here's a list of things to consider

◆ Pack a CD-ROM or other removable data storage device that contains your handouts and all relevant workshop materials. In the event that your printed materials do not reach the workshop location, you have the electronic files on this data storage device for reprinting.

◆ Pack the proper power cords, a spare battery for the laptop, and a bulb for the LCD or overhead projector in the event that these items are not available at the workshop location. This will require obtaining the make and model of all audiovisual and electronic equipment from the client during your planning process.

◆ Take an extension cord.

◆ Take reference materials, books, article reprints, and ancillary material. As a facilitator, you will occasionally have cause to refer to materials other than your own for additional information. Having the materials with you not only provides correct information about authors and articles; it also adds a positive reinforcement to participants' impression of your knowledge and training.

◆ Pack toys and games for the workshop, a timer or bell, and extra marking pens.

◆ Take duct tape! You may have to use this to tape extension cords to the floor as a safety precaution. The strength of duct tape also ensures that any flipchart pages hung on walls (with permission) will hold fast. Or, worst-case scenario, the duct tape can be used to contain unruly participants!

You can ship these items to the workshop in advance, but if the mail is slow or the package doesn't arrive at all, you face a predicament.

Participant Materials

These materials are the tools that enable participants to learn efficiently throughout the workshop. They provide continuing references after the workshop has ended. The materials also attest to the facilitator's insight, experience, and planning.

Every class must have the materials specifically designed for it, not just pulled from a file with the claim that "one size fits all." It's very important to perform a participant needs analysis before embarking on the development of materials. (Refer to The Importance of Self-Preparation for the Facilitator, chapter 1, and Assessment 11–2: Participant Survey and Needs Analysis.) There are several kinds of participant materials. Let's take a look at your options:

◆ handouts

◆ PowerPoint presentations and overhead slide masters

◆ CD-ROMs

◆ workbooks

◆ videos

◆ toys for participatory activities

HANDOUTS

The development and "look" of your handouts are vital to help participants understand the information they convey. Because this workshop is centered on communication, prepare your handouts in a way that communicates clearly from the outset. To compile the handouts properly, first gather together all assessments, tools, training instruments, activities, and PowerPoint slides and arrange them in the order they appear in the workshop. Then bind them together in some fashion. There are several options for compiling your material, ranging from inexpensive to deluxe. The kind of binding is your choice—materials can be stapled, spiral bound, or gathered in a ring binder—but remember that a professional look is a key to success. Your choice of binding will depend on your budget for the project. Because first appearances count, provide a cover with eye-catching colors and appropriate graphics.

Using the materials provided in chapters 6 through 12 and on the CD, select the PowerPoint slides, learning activities, training instruments, tools, and assessments appropriate to your workshop. Consider printing no more than three slides per handout page to keep your content simple with sufficient white space for the participants to write their own notes. Use the learning objectives for each workshop to provide clarity for the participants at the outset. Remember to number the pages, to add graphics for interest (and humor), and to include tabs for easy reference if the packet of materials has multiple sections.

Some participants like to receive the handouts electronically before the workshop begins. You may want to email participants to determine if they would like to receive the handouts electronically.

POWERPOINT PRESENTATIONS AND OVERHEAD SLIDE MASTERS

When you use PowerPoint software as a teaching tool, be judicious in the number of slides that you prepare. In a scientific lecture, slides are usually a necessity for explaining formulae or results, but a communication workshop relies on interaction so keep the slide information simple. Also, do not include more than five or six bullet points per slide.

A message can be conveyed quickly through the use of simple graphics. For example, an illustration of two people in conversation may highlight interpersonal communication; a photo of a boardroom-style meeting may illustrate a group engaged in negotiation.

When you use PowerPoint ask yourself first, "What will a slide add to my presentation?" Ensure that the answer that comes back is "it will enhance the message." If slides are simply used to make the workshop look more sophisticated or technical, the process may not achieve the desired results.

It can be frustrating when an instructor shows a slide for every page that the participants have in front of them. The dynamics of the class are likely to disconnect. If the information you are teaching is in the handouts or workbook, work from those media alone and keep the workshop personally interactive.

CD-ROMS

A CD-ROM can be a useful tool for participants to take with them from the classroom. It's a quick and easy-to-use reference. At the back of this book you will find a CD that contains the learning materials contained here. You are not permitted to copy this CD, but it will serve as a prototype for you. The CD you create and give to your students will contain copies of the handouts and instructional material that you have customized for your workshop.

WORKBOOKS AND JOURNALS

A participant journal may be included in the binder with your handouts or it may be a separate entity. Throughout the workshop participants can assess their progress and advance their development by entering details of their personal learning in the journal. The benefit of this journal to participants is that they can separate their personal discoveries and development from the main workshop handouts and use this journal as an action plan if desired. (See Tool 12–2: Journal Pages for our suggested handout.)

VIDEOS

When you show a video in your workshop, ensure that the skills contained in it are up-to-date and that the video is no longer than 20 minutes. Provide questions that will lead to a discussion of the information presented.

TOYS AND NOISEMAKERS

Experienced facilitators understand the value of gadgets and games that advance the learning, provide a break from learning, or both.

Adults love to play. When their minds are open they learn quickly and effectively. Something as simple as tossing a rubber ball from person to person as questions are asked about elements studied can liven up the workshop and help people remember what they've learned.

Case studies and lively exercises accelerate learning. Bells and whistles are forms of communication; use them when you pit two teams against each other or to indicate the end of an activity.

Facilitator Responsibilities

If you have to travel to your workshop location and if you are not familiar with the room where you'll hold your training session and how it is set up, ask to see it as soon as you arrive. When you can visualize your room before you sleep, it will help you make a quick assimilation on training day.

Take note of any elements that are missing when you visit the room so that you can make calls to the business office right then or first thing the next morning, or call your client contact. The following is a list of tasks that you should do when you arrive at the workshop room:

- ◆ Look at the access to the room and note the location of restrooms and telephones.

- ◆ Check the room temperature on arrival. A temperature of 70–72 °F is considered comfortable.

- ◆ Inspect the room set-up. Is it as you requested?

- ◆ Inspect equipment and compatibility with your own equipment and materials. *Be certain you know how to use everything.*

- ◆ Decide if the lighting is adequate. Find the light switches.

- ◆ Check the location of wall power plugs and power strips.

- ◆ Walk the room and determine the best presenting places.

- ◆ Place a welcome message that confirms the workshop date and title where participants can see it upon arrival.

When everything is in place and ready for the session, it's time to review the "soft skills" portion of your responsibilities—that is, how you conduct the workshop and interact with participants. Here are some things to consider:

- ◆ "Respect and Respond" could be a facilitator's mantra. At all times respect the participants and respond in a timely manner.

- ◆ Learn participants' names at the beginning of the workshop. Focus on each participant, give a firm handshake, repeat the name in your greeting, then mentally write the name on the person's forehead. When you have time, survey the room and write down every name without looking at nametags or name tents on the tables.

◆ Manage the time. This is vital because it ensures that the goals will be met in the time allotted.

◆ Read the participants' body language so that you know when to pause and ask questions or to give them a stretch break.

◆ Answer questions fully and effectively. If you don't know an answer, open the question up to the participants or offer to get back to the questioner. Make a note to remind yourself to do so.

◆ Add a "parking lot" to the room—a large sheet of paper taped to one of the walls (use your own artistic prowess to draw a vehicle of some sort). When questions arise that are out of step with the current communication activity, ask the participant to write the question on a sticky-note and put it in the parking lot. When the current activity is completed, you can address the questions parked there.

◆ Control unruly participants through assertiveness of vocal tone and message. When appropriate, invite them to help you with tasks because frequently they just need to be more physically involved. If the unruliness gets out of hand, accompany the person out of the room to discuss the situation.

◆ Be sure to monitor a participant who is slower to assimilate the information. If time permits, give that trainee some one-on-one time with you.

◆ Keep your energy high. Inject humor wherever possible. Ensure the learning is taking root.

Welcome and Introduction

As previously mentioned, the start of a session is a crucial time in the workshop dynamic. How the participants respond to you, the facilitator, can set the mood for the remainder of the workshop.

It is important to get to the classroom early, at least 30 to 60 minutes before the class. This gives you time not only to set up the room if that has not already been done, but also to test the environment, the seating plan, the equipment, and your place in the room. When participants begin to arrive (and some of them come very early), be ready to welcome them. Don't be distracted with problems or issues; be free and available to them.

While they are settling in you can ask questions:

- ◆ How was your commute?

- ◆ Have you traveled far for this workshop?

- ◆ Was it easy to find this room?

- ◆ May I help you with anything?

An instructor who offers to assist a participant will get off to a very easy start with relationship building.

Because this is a communication workshop, communication should be constantly in evidence. Set up a flipchart, a whiteboard, or a slide carrying the name of the workshop, your name, the date, and the length of the session. You may wish to write a pithy statement on the welcome board—for example, "90 percent of the success in life is showing up." Put some candies at the participants' places. You might add a smiley-face item to convey warmth with your welcome.

Music helps the participants relax. Take a CD or DVD player. Play lively music for the opening and classical or smooth music for personal work time. Create flipchart pages that carry the session agenda, session goals, and a listing of break times and facilities. Hang these pages around the room for color and interest.

When the class has arrived and is settled, introduce yourself. Write a humorous introduction, if that's your style, because this will humanize you. Talk more about what you want to accomplish in the workshop than about your accomplishments. If you have a short biographical piece included in the handouts or in the workbook, it may serve as your personal introduction.

At the conclusion of your introduction, provide an activity in which participants can meet each other. Don't limit the time on this too much unless you have an extremely tight schedule. The more time participants spend getting to know each other at the beginning of the workshop, the more all of you will benefit as the session proceeds.

Responding to Questions

When participants are asking questions, they are engaged and interested. Your responses to questions will augment the learning atmosphere. The way in which you respond is extremely important. Not only will it provide the participant asking the question with expanded knowledge; the way the answer is given will model desirable communication skills. Answers that are evasive can disturb a class because they bring your credibility into question. Glib or curt answers are insulting. Lengthy responses break the rhythm of the class and often go off track. When dealing with questions, the value of effective communication is in hearing the question, answering the question asked, and moving on. Repeat questions so that all participants hear them. In addition, this can ensure that you have heard the question correctly.

However, don't rush to answer. Take time to let everyone absorb the information. When time is of the essence, don't be tempted to give long, complicated answers that embrace additional topics. Be courteous and clear. Check that your answer has been understood. Unless a question is one that has been referred to the parking lot, answer it at the time it is asked. Consider answering with analogies when they are appropriate because these often help explain challenging concepts.

When a participant asks a confrontational or negative question, handle it with dignity and do not become aggressive. It's helpful to ask open-ended questions of the participant to try to clarify the original question. For example, ask, "What do you mean by . . . ?" or "Which part of the activity do you find challenging?" This form of open-ended questioning requires additional accountability from the participant. The reason for the confrontation may have arisen from confusion about the information or the need to hear his or her own thoughts aloud. When you are calm and patient there is a greater chance that the altercation will be resolved. If the participant persists, you may wish to ask him or her to discuss the specifics in a private setting. The open-ended questioning technique can also be used for general questions from participants.

Some participants will enjoy being questioned because it gives them an opportunity to show their knowledge. Others will be reticent for fear of looking foolish if they don't know the answer. Because your trainees have unique styles and personalities, you should always set goals for asking questions: Will these questions test the participants' knowledge? Are these questions appropriate? Am I asking them in the style that suits the participant?

Effective questions that prompt answers are open-ended:

- ♦ What have you learned so far?

- ♦ How do you feel about this concept?

- ♦ How would you handle this situation?

Any question that begins with "what" or "how" promotes a more extensive answer. Questions that begin with "why"—as in "why do you think that way?"—can promote defensiveness.

Why Things Go Bad

When you are invited to teach a communications class, the assumption is that you will succeed. Credentials and credibility have been checked, intelligence and inspiration are expected, and experience in the topic is recognized. Therefore it would seem that the stage is set for a top-quality class experience. Unfortunately, this is not always the case. So why do things go bad? Let's address the elements.

If the room is not arranged in a style conducive to learning, it can stymie the flow of the workshop. Tables that are placed in a U-shape or a teaching style (six to eight participants at a round table) at which each participant has visible access to other participants, and to the facilitator, are vital.

If the temperature is too hot in the room, the participants will feel drowsy and uncomfortable. If it is cold, they will be too concerned about their own well-being to listen and learn. A temperature of 70–72 °F is ideal.

You set the mood and tone for the participants. Your attitude when the participants first arrive is paramount. Your welcome must be warm, your approach friendly and inviting, and there must be an appearance of calm and organization.

Participants must feel secure as soon as they arrive to begin a workshop. When you've provided an agenda and clear path of instruction at the outset, the participants will feel safe and synchronized. They need guidelines because they are in your hands and need to know what is expected of them.

If the participants are not given time to get to know each other early in the workshop process, they will lack the confidence and comfort to engage. Relaxed time for the participants to get to know each other will set the workshop off on the right foot. You should arrange not only an opening icebreaker exercise, but scatter participant-appropriate team building exercises throughout the course. A class works best when the energy is high. High energy comes from connected participants.

Another component that can go bad is the rhythm of the class. If you haven't injected enough balance between written and lecture instruction, the class will get bored and lose interest. Remember the different learning styles and personalities of the participants. A change of facilitation style every 20–25 minutes will stimulate learning.

The limelight-seeker can play havoc with the rhythm of the class. There is always one person who likes to dominate the conversation and thereby limits the learning process. You must use tact and skill to rein this person in without humiliating him or her in the eyes of the class. Class time must not be compromised for this person. It takes a firm but gentle hand to rule the classroom successfully. Try statements like "You have some great ideas. Could you write them up for us and hand them out at the next session?" or "Your time is as important as ours and we have a lot to cover. We really must move on." Then move on!

If you poorly estimate the amount of time needed for each teaching activity, and time management goes by the wayside, the participants will become resentful. It is imperative that you know how long each activity will take, including time for practice or extra questions from the participants. Time management is a large component of the success of a class.

Things go bad when equipment doesn't work, or when you're unsure how to operate it. Familiarize yourself with all audiovisual and electronic equipment. Carry your own laptop computer and LCD projector whenever possible. Also know simple things like the location of the switch to lower a screen or how to copy from electronic whiteboards. Your expertise makes participants feel more comfortable.

In summary, effective communication in the classroom requires focus on the participants, clear and concise delivery, effective materials, and efficient question answering techniques, all of which will save time and accelerate learning.

What to Do Next

- ◆ Make arrangements for a room in which to hold your workshop.

- ◆ Gather information about your participants—who they are, what jobs they do, what their workshop goals are, and any specific needs or desires you should accommodate to enhance their learning.

- ◆ Prepare a detailed timeline.

- ♦ Prepare dynamic handouts and slides for your session. Be sure to make enough copies of your ancillary materials to match the number of participants you expect.

- ♦ Prepare yourself to facilitate the workshop by familiarizing yourself with the content and materials you'll present and by making sure you know how to operate all audiovisual and electronic equipment you'll be using.

- ♦ Consider and plan for the responsibilities you have as a facilitator. Design your welcome and introduction. Identify potentially challenging aspects of the workshop and how you will overcome them.

- ♦ Prepare a list of questions that you expect to get from the participants about the material, and then answer them. This is a useful "dress rehearsal" for the workshop.

♦ ♦ ♦

Now it is time to move on to the evaluation segment. In chapter 5 you will learn the importance of measuring the results of your workshop. You will find ideas for evaluating the participants' learning, supported by assessments in chapter 11. In addition, there is an action plan for the participants that will allow them to personally evaluate their progress.

Evaluating Your Communication Skills Workshop

What's in This Chapter?

- Discussion of the three Ws of evaluation—why, what, and when

- Information on how to perform meaningful evaluations

- Discussion of follow-up evaluations and personal action plans

Why Evaluate Your Program?

Evaluation is feedback. It is the quickest, surest way for you, as the facilitator, to learn if the messages and instruction are reaching the participants and if the participants are absorbing the content. It is also important for you to evaluate the participants' rate of progress and learning. Answers to the questions you ask throughout the workshop will help you identify much of the progress, but these answers come from only a few of the participants at a time. They're not a global snapshot of the entire group's comprehension and skills mastery.

When you lead a workshop, the participants walk a fine line between retention and deflection of knowledge. Continuing evaluations ensure that learning is taking root. So what do you evaluate in a communication skills workshop, and how do you do it?

What to Evaluate and How to Do It

There are four aspects to an evaluation:

- learning comprehension

- skills mastery

- ◆ skills application

- ◆ facilitator effectiveness.

Learning comprehension checks that the participants understand and grasp the skills being taught (see Assessment 11–8: Learning Comprehension Level).

Skills mastery means that the participants are able to demonstrate their newly acquired knowledge by some activity, such as teaching a portion of a module to their fellow participants or delivering their interpretation of communication specifics to the class. See Assessment 11–9: Skills Mastery for a means of evaluating this.

Skills application is the real test. You may choose to substantiate this through role plays or group case studies. When the participants have the opportunity to verbally communicate the skills learned and to reach desired results through such application, then skills application is established. See Assessment 11–10: Skills Application for questions designed to evaluate this aspect.

Facilitator effectiveness needs to be evaluated to provide feedback on instructional design and delivery. If there is a flaw in the design or delivery of the workshop, participants will typically let you know, and future changes can be made to improve the workshop. See Assessment 11–7 for a course and facilitator evaluation.

Here are some questions that can be asked to determine each participant's level of learning comprehension:

1. Give a brief overview of your learning in this workshop. (Begin your phrases with "I have learned . . . ." This will assist you in focusing your responses.)

2. How/where will you apply this knowledge in your workplace?

3. Did you acquire this knowledge through lectures/practice/discussion or a combination of all methods?

4. Do you feel sufficiently confident to pass on this knowledge to your colleagues?

5. Are there any areas that will require additional learning for you to feel sufficiently confident?

Now let's look at some questions you can use to evaluate your trainees' skills mastery:

1. If you were asked to teach one skill in this workshop, which skill would it be?

2. What would your three key message points be for that skill?

3. Describe the steps you would take to instruct each message point (for example, lecture, group discussion, PowerPoint presentation, and so forth).

4. What methods would you use to ensure that your participants are comprehending your instruction?

5. Would feedback from your participants, both positive and negative, affect the development of your skills mastery? If yes, illustrate your response and the changes you would make.

And finally, let's consider some questions that identify participants' ability to apply the skills they've learned in the workshop:

1. Please describe a situation at your workplace where you could employ one specific communication skill from this workshop.

2. How would you introduce this skill to your colleagues?

3. How would you set goals to measure the improvement from this skill?

4. Describe the input and participation you would expect from your colleagues.

5. How would you exemplify mastery of the skill?

The questions above are designed for written answers so you can incorporate them into the take-away workbook you create. The questions concerning skills mastery and skills application could be set as homework if the workshop is longer than one day. Keep in mind that you will also reevaluate after each day of a multiday session.

Now let's look at some questions participants can answer to evaluate the workshop and your effectiveness regarding its design and delivery:

1. Did the workshop meet your expectations? If not, why not?

2. Was [name] an effective facilitator? If not, why not?

3. Were the materials appropriate and applicable?

4. Did the facilitator have a good understanding of the material?

5. Did the facilitator respond to questions and lead an interactive workshop?

6. What three skills will you take from this workshop?

7. Were there any elements you did not like?

8. How would you change this workshop?

9. Was this training worthwhile?

10. Would you invite this facilitator back to lead another workshop?

By obtaining feedback from the participants about the workshop, you can make changes and adjust the flow of the content and activities to improve its overall effectiveness.

Let's now look at other forms of evaluation.

ROLE PLAYS

Role plays are an effective tool for assessing learning comprehension. If two or more participants conduct a role play that reveals their understanding of the information, with an outcome that reflects that understanding, then it becomes a "live-feed," instantaneous learning for all.

 You must set up the role play carefully. It is often wise for you to be a part of the first role-play experience to show participants how it's done and to make them more comfortable with the activity. Ensure that you explain all the steps of the role play and the desired outcome. It is insightful to role-play a negative version first, followed by participant discussion; then role-play a positive aspect the second time. For example, if confrontational communication is the topic and the situation under discussion involves a line manager and his or her supervisor, first enact the role play using the verbal and body language that is causing the negative result. Discuss this as a class to identify the specific language that needs improvement. Then enact the role play again, this time using positive language.

Frequently it is helpful for a participant who has been on the receiving end of negative communication in his or her workplace to adopt the role of deliverer. Walking in the other person's shoes leads to a quicker understanding of the transaction. This positive role play should also be followed by whole-group discussion of the elements that worked. Participants can be invited to write about the process and its results to give them a real-life example to take back to the workplace.

PARTICIPANT PRESENTATIONS

You might ask a participant to present a module of learning to the workshop. This allows the facilitator to observe the participants from a different perspective—both as listeners and as presenters. Be ready to assist or to answer questions. For example, a participant may choose assertive communication as his or her module, and the specific issue on return to the workplace may be a request for promotion. The participant defines and delivers the steps required to ask for the promotion while the facilitator and other participants observe and evaluate the success of the approach and demonstration of confidence and assertiveness.

BALL TOSS

A quick method for evaluating a class's knowledge of the material presented is to ask the participants to form a standing circle. The facilitator throws out a soft rubber ball to an individual and asks a question about the previous learning activity. When the catcher gives the right answer, he or she throws the ball to another participant who answers another question. The facilitator can step out of this circle and let the participants ask as well as answer questions to review the skills as a group. Candy for all as a reward for contributions is always enjoyed by the participants.

JOURNALING

Keeping a journal is a quiet, introspective way for participants to get a grip on their learning. When you complete an activity, have everyone to take five minutes to write a summary of the skill just learned and then ask them to share what they've written with a partner. Invite the partner to correct and improve the material if necessary or appropriate.

When to Evaluate Your Program

As you can see from the recommendations above, you can evaluate how your trainees are grasping and using what they're learning at any time throughout the workshop, and you should do that as often as you can. Doing so keeps everyone on track, helps people realize and reveal what they haven't understood, and provides needed breaks and breathers throughout the course of study. Don't forget to provide time for participants to evaluate the overall workshop at the end of the session.

Participants' Follow-Up Evaluation

It is important for participants to build personal accountability into their training. This provides an opportunity for the training to "stick" after the workshop has concluded and participants have returned to their workplaces.

Participants can be invited to complete the Personal Action Plan for Improving Your Communication Skills (Training Instrument 5–1 on page 41). With this Personal Action Plan, participants review what they have learned and set goals for themselves, with timelines for completion. They can seal the plan in an envelope and give it to a trusted colleague. At some appointed time, the colleague will return the unopened envelope to the participant.

For example, if a participant's goal is to give feedback to someone in the workplace within one month after the completion of the workshop, receiving the Personal Action Plan serves as a reminder to do so.

Here are the participants' steps for using the Personal Action Plan as a reminder of goals set:

- ◆ Complete Training Instrument 5–1: Personal Action Plan at the workshop, including a stated goal (for example, to provide feedback to a colleague on a specific issue).

- ◆ At the end of the workshop, put the Personal Action Plan into an envelope and seal it. Be sure to label the outside of the envelope with your name, address, and the return date (for example, one month away).

- ◆ Exchange envelopes with another workshop participant, with a promise to send the envelope to the owner on the return date.

- ◆ On time, send the envelope to your workshop partner and receive yours.

- ◆ When you receive the envelope, open it and read the contents. Check to see if you have followed through with your intended actions.

The process becomes more effective if the recipient updates the results of the planned action (in this example, giving feedback), and adds new goals to the plan. Then he or she reseals it in the envelope and asks the colleague to return it at some specified time. Taking this approach ensures that the communication goals are constantly being brought to the attention of the participant.

Training Instrument 5–1
Personal Action Plan for Improving Your Communication Skills

Instructions: Complete this Personal Action Plan and place it in an envelope labeled with your name, address, and return date. Exchange envelopes with another workshop participant and agree to return the envelope on the appointed date.

Describe your three key learnings today:

1. _____

2. _____

3. _____

List three actions you will take to specifically improve your personal communication skills (for example, active listening, tone, attentiveness, and so forth):

1. _____

2. _____

3. _____

List three actions or areas you will work on to improve your interpersonal communication with others (for example, providing feedback, sharing honest and open communication, being genuine, and so forth):

1. _____

2. _____

3. _____

THE 30-DAY ACTION PLAN

Instructions: Choose the most important of the action items listed above. Write yourself a note identifying what you want to do and by what date:

What to Do Next

- Identify evaluation points throughout the workshop.

- Design and develop forms and activities to measure your trainees' command of the knowledge and skills covered in the workshop.

- Prepare a course evaluation form (or customize the one presented in Assessment 11–7).

- Develop a plan for follow-up evaluations of trainees' skills mastery and on-the-job application.

◆ ◆ ◆

In chapter 6 you will find the outline for planning a successful one-hour communications session. The chapter contains the objectives for the session, the materials required for you and the participants, and a sample agenda.

One-Hour Session: Communications Overview

Communication skills affect every aspect of our lives, from business to work to our personal interactions and relationships. Developing and using effective communication skills take practice. The training session described in this chapter presents a brief introduction to these skills and some opportunities to practice them.

A one-hour overview of communication provides an example of what can be learned in a longer workshop. It enables participants to sample the topic and it gives you, the facilitator, an opportunity to observe participants' learning styles, discover potential roadblocks, and streamline the process. When participants hear about learning and communication styles that are new and diverse, their journey to understanding begins.

Objectives of the One-Hour Session

The objectives for participants in the one-hour session are to

- discover the impact that communication has in the workplace

- understand the principles of effective communication

- identify personal learning and communication styles

- identify personal goals for enhanced communication.

Materials

There is a number of things you will need in order to be prepared to facilitate this workshop. The list below will help you prepare properly.

For the facilitator:

- ◆ Projector, screen, and computer for running the PowerPoint presentation
- ◆ PowerPoint slides 6–1 through 6–12 (*One-hour.ppt* on the CD). Thumbnail versions of these slides appear at the end of this chapter.
- ◆ Learning Activity 10–1: Icebreaker: Getting to Know You
- ◆ Learning Activity 10–2: Understanding Yourself
- ◆ Flipchart and marking pen

For participants:

- ◆ Copies of PowerPoint slides 6–1 through 6–12 to be used as a workshop handout. Black-and-white versions of the slides can be printed from the overhead masters file, *One-Hour.pps,* located on the CD. (We recommend that you print three slides per page.)
- ◆ Training Instrument 10–1: The Circle of Influence
- ◆ 3 x 5-inch note cards

Using the CD

To access the electronic files, insert the CD and click on the appropriate Adobe .pdf document. Further directions and help in using the files can be found in the workbook appendix, "Using the Compact Disc."

Sample Agenda

The times assigned to the elements of this training are approximate and will vary with discussion and facilitator emphasis.

8:00 a.m.   Welcome and introduction (3 minutes)

Show PowerPoint slide 6–1. Welcome the participants; introduce yourself and the purpose of the one-hour session. Be sure to point out locations of restrooms, refreshments, and so on.

8:03 Discussion of agenda (5 minutes)

Show PowerPoint slide 6–2. Explain that during this hour participants will have the opportunity to learn the five principles of effective communication, practice one communication skill, identify how communication styles differ among participants, and identify personal communication goals for a half-day or full-day workshop.

8:08 Learning Activity 10–1: Icebreaker: Getting to Know You (15 minutes)

Show PowerPoint slide 6–3. Explain that sharing personal information begins the process of achieving effective communication. The additional step of introducing a partner to the other participants provides a comfortable connection.

8:23 Five principles of effective communication instruction (20 minutes)

Show PowerPoint slides 6–4 through 6–9. Explain the five principles, giving examples and descriptions of the skills required to begin effective communication.

Note: It's important that you review all of the slides as part of your preparation for the workshop. At that time you should plan explanations and examples for concepts presented in the slides.

8:43 Learning Activity 10–2: Understanding Yourself (10 minutes)

Show PowerPoint slide 6–10 and pass out a copy of Training Instrument 10–1 (or direct participants' attention to it in the packet of materials you prepared for them). On the flipchart, draw the Circle of Influence portrayed in Training Instrument 10–1.

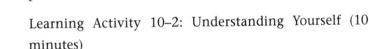

Inform attendees that they will be asked to reflect on the influences in their lives that have made them who they are today.

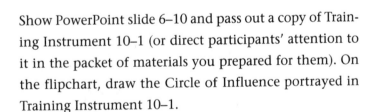

It is helpful if you model the process first. The center circle is "you" and the surrounding circles represent the various life experiences that have shaped your character, such as education, family, religion, culture, activities, and so forth.

Instruct the group to take a few minutes to consider for themselves their major life influences and note them on Training Instrument 10–1.

After the participants have completed the diagram, divide them into pairs and ask them to share what they are comfortable sharing with their partners. Assure them that they won't have to share this with the large group.

You can debrief this exercise with the large group by asking the following questions:

◆ What insights do you have about yourself after this exercise?

◆ Do your life experiences affect how you view others?

◆ How will the awareness of your biases affect your interaction with others?

The main point of this exercise is to make clear that we all view life through the filter of our own experiences, and that it is important to be aware of our biases so that we can improve our communication with others.

8:53   Individual goal setting (5 minutes)

Show PowerPoint slide 6–11. Hand out 3 x 5-inch note cards and ask each participant to write three goals for improved communication. (Responses might include more focused listening skills, increased awareness of appropriate body language, or questions to clarify indistinct communication.)

8:58   Summary, conclusion, and evaluation (2 minutes)

Show PowerPoint slide 6–12. Conclude the session with a summary of the points covered. Suggest ways in which participants can pursue the goals they wrote on their cards (for example, discuss with a supervisor, keep until the extended workshop is planned and work on them there, or follow up with the facilitator).

Upon completion of the workshop summary, distribute the session evaluation (Assessment 11–7) and ask the participants to complete it before they leave the room. Feedback from the participants can provide you with information to continuously improve your facilitation of the workshop.

What to Do Next

- ♦ Prepare for the one-hour workshop by investigating the needs of the participants. For example, find out what is each person's role in the organization, why is she or he attending the session, and what are the participant's or supervisor's goals for attendance at the workshop.

- ♦ Compile and review the learning activities, handouts, and slides you will use in this session.

- ♦ If the one-hour session is the "teaser" for a longer workshop (half-day, full-day, or two-day), be sure to know when the longer session will be presented. If the participants leave the one-hour session feeling hungry for further information and knowledge, they will be better satisfied with a next-step plan.

♦ ♦ ♦

Chapter 7 includes an agenda and learning activities for a half-day workshop. It offers a sample agenda, objectives for the workshop, and the opportunity to explore the learning in greater detail. Specific skills can be studied and practiced because of the longer timeframe.

Slide 6–1

Welcome to a One-Hour Overview of Effective Communication Skills

Name of Organization
Date
Facilitator Name

Slide 6–2

Agenda

- Welcome/icebreaker
- Five principles of effective communication
- Understanding yourself
- Goal setting
- Summary and close

Slide 6–3

Getting to Know You

Slide 6–4

Five Principles of Effective Communication

- Listen effectively.
- Respond appropriately.
- Read body language.
- Ask questions to clarify.
- Seek common ground.

Slide 6–5

Five Principles of Effective Communication

Listen Effectively

- Focus on the speaker.
- Shut out internal/external noise.
- Listen without bias.
- Affirm and acknowledge statements.
- Don't interrupt.

Slide 6–6

Five Principles of Effective Communication

Respond Appropriately

- Ask open-ended questions.
- Repeat and reflect.
- Don't judge.
- Be aware of your own biases.
- Be courteous.

Slide 6–7

Five Principles of Effective Communication

Read Body Language

- Be aware of your own body language.
- Look for body language that conflicts with the verbal message.
- Respond to changes in body posture.
- Model positive body language.

Slide 6–8

Five Principles of Effective Communication

Ask Questions to Clarify

- Focus on the topic.
- Begin with "how" or "what."
- Remember that "why" can cause defensiveness.
- Clarify the feeling behind the words.
- Use the speaker's words.

Slide 6–9

Five Principles of Effective Communication

Seek Common Ground

- Use similar verbal and body language.
- Respect and reflect.
- Seek a win–win solution.
- Check that all parties understand.
- Compromise is better than conflict.

Slide 6–10

Understanding Yourself

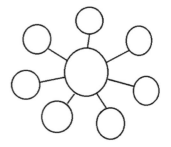

Slide 6–11

Setting Goals

Three goals for improved communication

1 _____

2 _____

3 _____

Slide 6–12

Summary and Close

- Five principles of effective communication
- Understand yourself and how you communicate
- Review your goals

Half-Day Communication Skills Workshop

- Objectives for the half-day communication skills workshop
- List of materials for the facilitator and the participants
- Sample program agenda

The opportunities in a half-day workshop extend considerably beyond those offered by a one-hour overview because participants have time to explore their personal goals, practice two communication skills, and develop interpersonal relationships with their colleagues. There is also time for participants to ask questions and discuss different perspectives and skills.

Objectives of the Half-Day Session

The objectives for participants in the half-day session are to

- study and practice two strategies of effective communication:
    - listening skills
    - body language
- discover how to handle both individual and group communication challenges
- identify personal areas for improvement.

Materials

There are a number of things you will need to put together in order to be prepared to facilitate the workshop. The list below will help you prepare properly.

For the facilitator:

- Projector, screen, and computer for running the PowerPoint presentation

- PowerPoint slides 7–1 through 7–24 (*Half-Day.ppt* on the CD)

- Learning Activity 10–3: Icebreaker: Life Is Just a Bowl of Candies

- Learning Activity 10–4: The Listening Stick

- Learning Activity 10–5: Active Listening Role Play

- Learning Activity 10–6: Visual Listening

- Learning Activity 10–7: One on One

- Soft ball

- Bowl filled with wrapped candies (avoid those with nuts and include sugar-free ones; have several for each participant)

- Flipchart and marking pen

For the participants:

- Copies of PowerPoint slides 7–1 through 7–24 to be used as a workshop handout. Black-and-white versions of the slides can be printed from the overhead masters file, *Half-Day.pps,* on the CD. (We suggest that you print three slides per page.)

- Tool 12–2: Journal Pages

- Tool 12–3: Tips for Understanding Body Language

- Tool 12–4: One on One

- Assessment 11–4: Listening Skills

- Assessment 11–7: Course and Facilitator Evaluation

Using the CD

Materials for this training session are provided in this workbook and as electronic files on the accompanying CD. To access the electronic files, insert the CD and click on the appropriate Adobe .pdf document. Further directions and help using the files can be found in the appendix, "Using the Compact Disc," at the back of this workbook.

It's important that you review all of the slides as part of your preparation for the workshop. At that time you should plan explanations and examples for concepts presented in the slides.

Sample Agenda

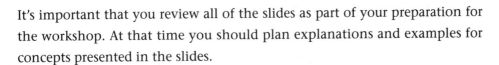

The times assigned to the elements of this training are approximate and will vary with discussion and facilitator emphasis.

8:00 a.m.   Welcome and introduction (5 minutes)

Show PowerPoint slide 7–1. Welcome the participants; introduce yourself and the purpose of the half-day workshop. Ensure that everyone knows where restrooms and vending machines are located. Check the room temperature with participants.

8:05   Discussion of agenda (5 minutes)

Show PowerPoint slide 7–2. Review the objectives for the workshop and answer questions from the participants.

8:10   Icebreaker: Learning Activity 10–3 (10 minutes)

Show PowerPoint slide 7–3. Pass around the bowl of candies and ask everyone to take as many candies from the bowl as they would like (without telling them why). Ask them to count the candies they've taken.

Choose a starting point and have each participant tell one fact about himself or herself for every candy he or she took.

8:20   Personal goals (15 minutes)

Show PowerPoint slide 7–4. Distribute the journal pages (Tool 12–2), and ask participants to write their personal goals for the workshop on the journal page. Then ask each participant to read aloud his or her goals, and as this is done, write them on the flipchart so that they are visible during the workshop. This helps you support goal achievement because the goals are easily accessible.

8:35 Basics of listening (10 minutes)

Show PowerPoint slide 7–5. This slide lists the five levels of listening:

◆ Element 1, ignoring, is the equivalent of nonlistening. Someone is speaking but in the receiver there is no apparent signal that information is being received. Teenagers can be very good at this!

◆ Element 2 is almost as negative as element 1. Pretending to listen is done by someone who is usually occupied in a task while listening. This person may utter sounds of agreement but would have difficulty if asked to reiterate the communication.

◆ Element 3, selective listening, is hearing only what one wants to hear. For example, if a young person is told "yes, you may borrow the car, but you must not carry any passengers," the youth may hear only the first half of the message and not the second. Selective listening can cause errors in personal and professional situations.

◆ Element 4, attentive listening, engages the visual and body language of the listener. The listener may nod or react to the message while making eye connection with the speaker. This listening will trigger a positive response in the speaker and allow a free flow of information.

◆ Element 5, empathic/active listening, is frequently referred to as "peak" listening. In this instance the listener is fully engaged with body language, physical language, and oral language. The listener reflects the speaker's key statements and asks open-ended questions that help the speaker feel confident and comfortable in the flow of communication. This listener will fully understand the message being delivered and will be able to act on it accordingly. The listener is seeking to understand the message and the messenger at that point in time. The listener also knows his or her own agenda in the transaction—that is, knows where not to cross a line of confidence into a counseling role.

Listening actively is a choice. When it is made, the people involved in the communication exchange benefit from the deep level of understanding that is reached.

8:45   Basics of listening, continued (5 minutes)

Show PowerPoint slide 7–6, review the basics of listening, and present the idea that listening is a choice. You can make the point that one must first care enough to take the time to really focus on the other person, without bias.

8:50   Basic listening role play (15 minutes)

Show PowerPoint slide 7–7. Use the role plays below to demonstrate the application of these skills.

Ask two participants to role-play a scenario in which they assume the roles of a supervisor and a subordinate. The subordinate's goal is to receive a pay increase. The supervisor will adopt the negative listening technique of pretending to listen.

When the role play is complete, discuss it as a class and identify the negative areas that need improvement and change. Was the subordinate heard? Would there be a pay raise or action taken toward a pay raise?

Then replay the scenario (selecting two different participants is often beneficial). The supervisor in this role play will use active/empathic listening.

Ask the questions you asked after the first role play to identify the outcome of the communication, and discuss the outcome as a group.

9:05   Learning Activity 10–4: The Listening Stick (10 minutes)

Show PowerPoint slide 7–8. Describe the exercise in Learning Activity 10–4. Participants perform the exercise in pairs and then regroup to discuss the experience. The discussion points included in the learning activity will help you debrief the activity.

Refer to Tool 12–2: Journal Pages and suggest that everyone capture the discoveries they made during the exercise.

9:15   Break (15 minutes)

9:30   Review of skills (5 minutes)

When participants return from a break, it is useful to spend a short time reviewing the previous learning. Toss a ball to one participant at a time and ask a question about the information or skills already explored. Tell each catcher to toss the ball back to you when he or she has given an answer. (This question-and-answer process gives you insight into how well trainees are assimilating knowledge.)

9:35   More basics of listening (15 minutes)

Show PowerPoint slides 7–9 and 7–10 to present examples of "traditional" and active/empathic listening.

Using the six bullets on slide 7–9, divide participants into as many groups as needed to give each group one bullet point to consider. Ask groups to use a flipchart page to note their thoughts and discussion points. A spokesperson from each group will present the group's findings to the whole class for discussion.

Show slide 7–10 and introduce the concept of active/empathic listening. Explain that active listening skills will not be effective unless they come from a sincere desire to understand, and that these skills must be built one step at a time. The establishment of trust is the key point because it promotes the growth of a positive relationship.

Explain that active listening will be covered in more detail following the next activity.

9:50   Assessment 11–4: Listening Skills (15 minutes)

Show PowerPoint slide 7–11 and distribute Assessment 11–4. Ask the participants to complete the assessment honestly and to identify three key elements for improvement.

Following the completion of the assessment, ask everyone to find a partner with whom to discuss their thoughts about the questions, their answers, and the areas they'd like to improve. Allow five minutes for the discussion, and ask the participants to add their thoughts to their personal journals (Tool 12–2).

10:05   Principles of active listening (15 minutes)

When Assessment 11–4 has been completed, ask participants to put it aside while you introduce slides 7–12 through 7–15. Illustrate the examples of active and empathic listening that enable the listener to get inside the speaker's head to interpret the messages and to ask appropriate questions.

Show PowerPoint slide 7–12, Principles of Active Listening. Present the ideas of *repeat, rephrase, reflect,* and *rephrase and reflect.* Explain that being truly skilled at active listening takes a lot of practice. It is also important to know when to use active listening appropriately.

For example, it is more appropriate to use active listening for difficult situations when clear communication and understanding are imperative. It is not appropriate to use active listening for most casual or informal conversations. Explain the four principles of active listening:

1. **Repeat:** This is the first-stage skill in empathic listening. By repeating what someone says, you show that you're paying attention.

2. **Rephrase:** At this more effective stage you restate what was said in your own words. It involves thinking about the other person's statements and processing what was actually said.

3. **Reflect:** This stage focuses on the feeling behind the words, not just what is being said. You mirror what you are sensing from the speaker.

4. **Rephrase and Reflect:** This is where trust is built. When you rephrase the content and reflect the feeling, others will sense your desire to really listen and understand what is being said.

This process provides the opportunity for clarification if there is a misinterpretation or miscommunication, and it can lead to problem resolution as communication on an issue becomes more and more clear.

Show PowerPoint slides 7–13 through 7–15. These slides explain the reasons for rephrasing and give specific examples of rephrasing and paraphrasing. The point to stress here is the importance of communicating an understanding of the emotion involved in the speaker's message.

10:20

Learning Activity 10–5: Active Listening Role Play (20 minutes)

Show PowerPoint slide 7–16 and refer to Learning Activity 10–5. The active listening role play is a great way to give participants some brief practice.

Ask the participants to form pairs and choose a work-related topic to discuss. One person in the pair talks about the topic for five minutes while the other person practices active listening. After five minutes, partners exchange roles.

Discuss the exercise as a whole group to ensure that participants have experienced the benefits of full and active listening. When debriefing this activity, one of the main points is to call attention to how five minutes seems to pass quickly when listening is active. Point out how this differs from the experience of time in the Listening Stick activity, when one minute seemed much longer. Active listening takes the commitment of time.

10:40   Journaling (5 minutes)

Following the exercise, ask participants to look at their responses to items on Assessment 11–4 and review the three elements they will work on when they return to the workplace. Ask them to transfer these elements, along with the active or empathic listening principles they will implement, to their journal pages (Tool 12–2).

10:45   Stretch break (5 minutes)

10:50   Basics of body language (20 minutes)

Show PowerPoint slides 7–17 and 7–18. Explain that open, confident body language constitutes approximately 50 percent of all communication. What we say is underlined by our body language. Therefore, to be effective, body and voice should be in harmony when communicating.

Role-play using Tool 12–3: Tips for Understanding Body Language and the information on slides 7–17 and 7–18 to highlight these physical communication skills.

Using slide 7–18, ask two volunteers to role-play a negative body language encounter. The participants will create the characters and dialogue in the role play (for example, one volunteer might become a senior manager, the other an opinionated recent graduate looking for a job). Discuss the role play as a whole group. Then ask for two new volunteers to take the same roles and use positive body language. Discuss the outcome from this role play with the whole group.

11:10   Journaling (5 minutes)

Ask participants to spend five minutes writing about the importance that positive body language will have with a specific colleague when they return to the workplace.

11:15

Vocal emphasis (10 minutes)

Show PowerPoint slide 7–19. Explain that when we make judgments while listening, our attitude will reflect these judgments. The judgments can be caused by a variety of biases we may have—gender, culture, age, or simply our opinion of the speaker.

Show PowerPoint slide 7–20 and explain that the next lesson reveals how the use of voice tone and point of emphasis can change a message significantly.

First, read the sentence "I didn't steal your cow yesterday" without emphasis on any particular word.

Then read the sentence again, emphasizing the word "I" and varying your body language. Ask the participants what the sentence means.

Repeat the sentence four more times, each time emphasizing a different word—"steal," "your," "cow," "yesterday"—and changing your body language. After each repetition, ask the class to explain what the sentence means.

Use the following questions to prompt discussion among the participants:

◆ How many meanings can you get from one sentence?

◆ What other words or phrases can be interpreted in different ways?

11:25

Visual listening (10 minutes)

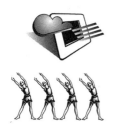

Show PowerPoint slide 7–21 and conduct Learning Activity 10–6: Visual Listening. Ask participants to select a partner and put their chairs back to back. Each person's task is to describe the partner's physical image (clothing/features/body language). Partners then turn and check how correctly they described one another. This exercise makes participants aware of their shortcomings (or successes) in observing others.

11:35   Case study in communication (15 minutes)

Show PowerPoint slide 7–22 and pass out copies of Tool 12–4: One on One. Ask participants to form groups of four or five people. Ask a volunteer from each group to read aloud the study in Tool 12–4.

After the study has been read, each group will discuss the study based on the debriefing questions in Learning Activity 10–7.

11:50   Goal setting (5 minutes)

Show PowerPoint slide 7–23 and ask participants to review the journal notes they made throughout the workshop. Then ask them to summarize their key goals for improving their communication skills. This is a great opportunity for them to focus on key skills they hope to develop.

11:55   Summary and close (5 minutes)

Show PowerPoint slide 7–24. Ask for final questions, comments, and contributions. Review the initial goals from the beginning flipchart to determine if the participants have met them. Address any questions that arise.

Distribute the workshop evaluation (Assessment 11–7) for the participants to complete. Conclude the workshop by thanking the participants for their involvement. Tell them it has been a pleasure for you to work with them. Shake hands with participants as you say farewell to them.

What to Do Next

- ◆ Work with the organization to identify the workshop participants and establish the workshop schedule. (We recommend no more than 20 attendees.)

- ◆ Notify participants of the workshop schedule.

- ◆ Visit the workshop location to make a visual assessment of the facility. This helps you in planning the room set-up and layout.

- ◆ Prepare for the half-day workshop by reviewing the workshop objectives and becoming fully conversant with the content of the slides and other materials. Be sure you are ready to answer questions that arise from group discussions.

- ◆ Check your agenda to ensure that you have allotted enough time for each activity.

- ◆ Compile the learning activities, handouts, and slides you will use in this session.

- ◆ Prepare any ancillary articles you may take with you to the workshop to clarify specific points or answer participants' questions (for example, journal articles and Web links).

◆ ◆ ◆

The next chapter offers great opportunity for a broader and deeper study of communication skills in a full-day workshop. It includes objectives, materials, and a sample agenda.

Slide 7–1

Welcome to a
Half-Day Workshop on
Effective Communication Skills

Name of Organization
Date
Facilitator's Name

Slide 7–2

Agenda

- Welcome and introduction
- Goal setting
- Study and practice the five levels of listening
- Discover the basics of listening
- Understand and practice active listening
- Identify and practice appropriate body language
- Clarify tone and attitude – it's not *what* you say
- Practice visual listening
- Identify your personal areas for progress

Slide 7–3

Life Is Just a Bowl of Candies

Enjoy
Yourself!

Slide 7–4

Personal Goals

- What do you want to learn today?
- What tools do you want to take back to the workplace?
- What do you need to help you improve?

Use your journal to capture these thoughts.

Slide 7–5

Basics of Listening

Five Levels

- Ignoring
- Pretending
- Selective
- Attentive
- Empathic/Active

Seek to Understand

- Listen to understand
- Clarify the message
- Be understood
- Be open to other points of view
- Know your agenda

Slide 7–6

Basics of Listening

Recognize that listening is not simply waiting for your turn to talk.

Listening Is a Choice

- Decide that you want to listen.
- Listen with a clean slate.
- Clean your filter regularly.

Slide 7–7

Listening Stick Activity

It takes time
to listen!

Use your journal to capture these thoughts.

Slide 7–8

Basics of Listening

Traditional/Nonempathic Listening

- Listening – with the intent to reply
- Filtering – through your own agenda
- Evaluating – do you agree or disagree?
- Probing – asking from your frame of reference
- Advising – counseling on the basis of your experience
- Interpreting – trying to figure it out

Slide 7–9

Basics of Listening

Active/Empathic Listening

- Desire to fully understand
- Build one step at a time
- Create trust and a positive relationship

Slide 7–10

Basic Listening Role Play

Slide 7–11

Assess Your Listening Skills

- Complete the Listening Skills Assessment. Be honest!
- Identify three key elements for improvement.
- Discuss these key elements with a partner.

When you journal, add these elements.

Slide 7–12

Principles of Active/Empathic Listening

- **Repeat.** This shows you are paying attention.
- **Rephrase.** Think about the other person's agenda.
- **Reflect.** Respond to both message and feelings.
- **Rephrase and reflect.** Build trust.

Slide 7–13

Examples of Active Listening

Why Rephrase?

- To clarify understanding
- To gain more information
- To move toward the answer/action/solution

Slide 7–14

Examples of Active Listening

Paraphrasing:

- "What I am hearing you say is ___. Is that right?"
- "In other words, you ___ [think, feel that] . . . ."
- "It sounds as if you're saying ___."
- Let me make sure I've got this right. You ___."

Slide 7–15

Examples of Active Listening

Empathy Guidelines – empathy expresses how you think the other person feels and why. It conveys understanding and builds a connection. It does not mean you agree or feel the same way.

Examples:

- "It sounds as if you feel ___ *[feeling]*, because ___ *[reason].*"
- "It must be ___ *[feeling]* when ___ *[reason].*"
- "I can understand that ___ *[reason]* would make you ___ *[feeling].*"

Slide 7–16

Active Listening Role Play

- Find a partner.
- Select a work-related challenge to discuss.
- One person talks; the other listens and applies active listening techniques.
- Exercise gives five minutes to each speaker.
- Swap roles.
- Regroup to debrief.

Use your journal to capture these thoughts.

Slide 7–17

Basics of Body Language

➢ **Be present with your whole body**
 – Extend an open invitation to conversation.
 – Acknowledge messages from others.
 – Mirror; don't mimic.

  ➢ **Signs**
  - Gestures
  - Posture
  - Eye contact
  - Movement

Slide 7–18

Basics of Body Language

- **Tightly folded arms and crossed feet:** Skeptical/defensive*
- **Chin stroking:** Making a decision
- **Fist on cheek, index finger pointing upward:** Listening with interest
- **Hands clasped at chin, elbows on table:** Defensive/evaluating
- **Rubbing hands together:** Excitement/optimism
- **Hand over mouth:** Skepticism, evaluation, or suppressing deceit
- **Chewing tips of fingers:** Anxiety

* This language is also used when the person is feeling cold, so be cautious with your interpretation.

Slide 7–19

Your Voice Reflects Your Listening

➤ **Listen to what is and is not said.**
· Respond first to the feeling, then to the content.
· Be aware of your emotional involvement.
· Remember that the same statement can have several interpretations.

➤ **Your attitude comes across.**
· Be mindful in your word choice and emphasis.
· Avoid sexist, racist, and other inappropriate words.
· Treat others with dignity and respect.

Slide 7–20

Vocal Emphasis

I didn't
steal
your
cow
yesterday

Slide 7–21

Visual Listening

- Choose a partner.
- Sit back-to-back.
- Take 90 seconds each to describe your partner's physical appearance (clothing, features, and so on).
- Also include observations about your partner's body language.
- Regroup to debrief.

Use your journal to capture these thoughts.

Slide 7–22

Evaluating a Case Study

One on One (Employee – Boss)

Slide 7–23

Goal Setting

- _____
- _____
- _____
- _____
- _____

Remember to define realistic goals.

Use your journal to capture these thoughts.

Slide 7–24

Summary and Close

- Five levels of listening
- Basics of listening
- Active/empathic listening
- Body language
- Tone and attitude
- Visual listening
- Personal areas for progress

Full-Day Communication Skills Workshop

What's in This Chapter

- Objectives for the full-day communication skills workshop

- List of materials for the facilitator and the participants

- Sample program agenda

A full-day workshop provides an excellent opportunity to explore more fully several communication skills or focus on one skill that is creating challenges in the workplace. Participants can relax with each other and study the topics in more depth. As the facilitator, you have more time to instruct and expand on a skill. At the end of a full-day workshop, trainees frequently continue their conversations when back in the workplace, which further promotes connection and enhanced communication.

It is a well-reported statistic that adults learn best when the learning activities change every 20 to 25 minutes. Therefore, plenty of variety is needed in a day-long format.

In the activities we've put together for this full-day workshop we outline different paradigms in communication, explore interpersonal communication and its applications in the workplace, discuss the impact of conflict in communication and how to resolve it, provide strategies for persuasion and negotiation in communication, and provide key guidelines for giving and receiving feedback. The agenda contains all the elements you'll need to facilitate a successful full-day workshop, but we recommend that you decide which topics are most appropriate to meet your participants' needs and choose your activities carefully to create the most effective full-day workshop possible.

Objectives of the Full-Day Session

The participants' objectives in the full-day session are to

- ◆ understand different paradigms in communication

- ◆ explore interpersonal communication and its applications

- ◆ explore the impact of conflict in communication, and how to resolve it

- ◆ study strategies for persuasion and negotiation in communication

- ◆ develop strategies for giving and receiving feedback.

Materials

There are a number of things you will need to put together to be prepared to facilitate the workshop. The list below will help you prepare properly.

For the facilitator:

- ◆ Projector, screen, and computer for running the PowerPoint presentation

- ◆ PowerPoint slides 8–1 through 8–26 (*Full-Day.ppt* on the CD)

- ◆ Learning Activity 10–8: Icebreaker: Class Reunion

- ◆ Learning Activity 10–9: Interpersonal Skills

- ◆ Learning Activity 10–10: I Want It!

- ◆ Learning Activity 10–11: Ten Questions About Conflict

- ◆ Learning Activity 10–12: Persuasion

- ◆ Learning Activity 10–13: Persuasion Strategy

- ◆ Learning Activity 10–14: Negotiation Outcomes

- ◆ Learning Activity 10–15: Feedback Experience

- ◆ Learning Activity 10–16: Johari Window

- ◆ Rubber ball

- ◆ Flipchart and marking pen

For the participants:

- Copies of PowerPoint slides 8–1 through 8–26 to be used as a workshop handout. Black-and-white versions of the slides can be printed from the overhead masters file, *Full-Day.pps,* on the CD. (We suggest that you print three slides per page.)

- Tool 12–2: Journal Pages

- Tool 12–5: Maslow's Hierarchy of Needs

- Tool 12–6: Nonconfrontational Language—Using "I" Rather Than "You"

- Tool 12–7: Skills for Interpersonal Success

- Tool 12–8: Pointers for Developing Interpersonal Skills and the Benefits of Doing So

- Tool 12–9: Five Steps to Resolving Conflict

- Tool 12–10: Persuasion Guidelines

- Tool 12–11: Negotiation Strategies

- Tool 12–12: Simple Guidelines for Giving Feedback

- Training Instrument 10–2: Feedback Questionnaire

- Training Instrument 10–3: Johari Window

- Assessment 11–5: Interpersonal Skills

- Assessment 11–6: Negotiation Skills and Readiness

- Assessment 11–7: Course and Facilitator Evaluation

- Toys such as squeeze balls, Lego® blocks, pipe cleaners, or Play-Doh®. (Some people like to keep their hands busy because it helps them focus their listening, and these toys give them the opportunity to do so.)

- Sticky notes

- 3 x 5-inch note cards

- Paper and pens

- Flipcharts and marking pens (one set for each group of four trainees)

Using the CD

Materials for this training session are provided in this workbook and as electronic files on the accompanying CD. To access the electronic files, insert the CD and click on the appropriate Adobe .pdf documents. Further directions and help using the files can be found in the appendix, "Using the Compact Disc," at the back of this workbook.

It's important that you review all of the slides as part of your preparation for the workshop. At that time you should plan explanations and examples for concepts presented in the slides.

Preparation

Create posters with messages like "Successful Communication Is the Key to Success" or "90 Percent of Success in Life Is Just Showing Up" (in this case, for the workshop). Use some of your favorite quotes about communication. You might want to create a poster with examples of active verbs (see Tool 12–1). It will serve as a vocabulary resource for participants. Be sure to use color on the posters to create a dynamic atmosphere for learning. When participants enter the room, some are nervous. Images and messages give them something to look at and read, and that helps them forget their nervousness.

Before the participants arrive, put toys, Play-Doh, and pads of sticky notes on the tables. Hang the posters on the walls where they'll be easily noticed. If you bring a CD player to the room, have music playing while the participants enter. Music relaxes people and provides an undercurrent of comfort.

Sample Agenda

The times assigned to the elements of this training are approximate and will vary with discussion and facilitator emphasis.

8:00 a.m. Welcome and introduction (5 minutes)

Show PowerPoint slide 8–1. Welcome the participants; introduce yourself and the purpose of the full-day workshop. Ensure that everyone knows where restrooms and vending machines are located and where they can get lunch. Check the room temperature with class members, and adjust if necessary.

8:05   Discussion of agenda (10 minutes)

Show PowerPoint slides 8–2 and 8–3. Also write the agenda on a flipchart page that will be visible all day. Go through the agenda with participants and answer any questions.

8:15   Icebreaker: Learning Activity 10–8 (10 minutes)

Show PowerPoint slide 8–4. Explain that this activity will help participants create energy and enthusiasm in the room. After you explain the two parts of the icebreaker, recommend that they not overwhelm the other participants in the second part of the activity, but note that the warmer their greeting, the more learning will take place.

8:25   Goal setting and individual introductions (20 minutes)

Show PowerPoint slides 8–5 and 8–6 and pass out note cards to all trainees. Invite the participants to write their goals on the cards and to lay the cards face-up in front of them. You may choose to write all of the goals on the flipchart as well.

Instruct everyone to exchange cards with a person next to them and then to ask any two things about that person (for example, where were you born and raised? what's your favorite food? do you have children?). Give enough time for the class to accomplish this exchange of information. Then have each person introduce the class member he or she questioned, being sure to tell what two facts have been learned and to read aloud that person's goals.

8:45   Communication paradigms (15 minutes)

Show PowerPoint slides 8–7 and 8–8. Using the following information, lead a general discussion from these slides, eliciting comments and questions from participants.

Paradigms are typical examples of a theory or idea that is generally understood. In communication, these paradigms cover the common or regular uses of exchanges between people, either individually or in groups. For example, when giving directions to a location in your city, the assumption is made that you know the way: therefore we are operating from the same paradigm.

◆ **Know your frame of reference:** This means understanding the big-picture situation before embarking on interpersonal discussion or perhaps conflict resolution. Participants should ask themselves the following questions: Who are the players? What is the issue? What is the expected outcome? Why have issues not been resolved in the past? What is my role? Are there any boundaries I shouldn't cross?

◆ **Why is the information being exchanged?** What is the purpose of this communication exchange? What will change or not change as a result of the interaction? What results are expected and do they differ for both parties in the discussion?

◆ **What does the recipient need from you?** For the initiator of the communication it is very important to understand what is required by the other party. Does the recipient need answers to questions? Is the recipient requesting a decision from you? Is the recipient looking for guidance, counseling, or advice? How does the recipient like to receive information (directly and succinctly or in a more detailed form)?

◆ **What do you need from the recipient?** Asking this question helps the participant be very clear to himself or herself before the communication exchange. Do I need an answer or decision from the recipient? Do I need permission for an action from the recipient? Do I need buy-in or accountability? Do I need follow-up information?

◆ **How will the information affect status?** When a participant enters a contentious dialogue with a more senior colleague, the forthrightness of the communication frequently can affect status. For example, if a participant approaches a supervisor with information that may shed a negative light on the supervisor, there could be a confrontational exchange with resulting difficulty for the participant. Here are questions the participant should ask before entering the exchange: What are the risks involved in this communication exchange? What might I lose as a result of this interaction? What might I gain as a result of the exchange? How might my relationship with my supervisor change as a result of my honesty and risk?

◆ **Is the organizational hierarchy in play?** This question relates directly to the one above it. If the participant is employed in an organization that adheres strictly to a formal hierarchy where supervisors have the final say in decision making, then a contentious communication exchange poses risks for the participant. Either style could cause problems if there is a strong hierarchy. Some questions to ask before the interaction are these: Do I fully understand the hierarchy of my organization? What have I observed in other exchanges that I can learn from? How open and honest is my communication with my supervisor? What results might I expect from crossing a hierarchical boundary?

◆ **Is the information being received through a confrontational filter?** When a recipient in a communication exchange expects confrontation, boundaries are frequently already in place. A participant may meet resistance at the outset of the dialogue or discover that decisions have already been made before the communication encounter takes place. A participant should therefore ask the following questions: Do I have a challenging relationship with the recipient that will make communication difficult? Have we had an experience similar to the one we will now embark on that will color any decisions? Should I invite a third party to be present at the communication exchange? Should I take detailed notes at the meeting?

◆ **Is everyone on the same map?** Here are the important questions for the participant to ask: Are we looking at the same picture and desirous of the same result? Do my personal or professional filters in communication drive me in one direction when I should be moving in another? Where are the recipient's communication filters pointed? Will we participate in this dialogue as team members or as separate entities? Do I have to convey specific information at the beginning of the communication to set the background and history?

By asking these questions, participants will be appropriately prepared before they enter a communication exchange and therefore more likely to be successful in the enterprise. In other words, they should diagnose before they can effectively prescribe.

9:00   Maslow's Hierarchy of Needs (10 minutes)

Show PowerPoint slide 8–9 and distribute Tool 12–5. Use this slide to illustrate the progress of our development as humans.

As we develop physically, our higher-level needs develop also. As babies we are satisfied with milk, simple toys, and love. As we continue in our development and growth we start asking for more interesting food, more complicated games and toys, and clothing that fits our specific style. We want to be like others in our peer groups. It is important for young children to fit the mold they see around them, at home and at school. We make these demands through our power of communication and the constant adherence to our hierarchy of needs that ultimately demand satisfaction.

The first two and most basic needs, physiological and safety, refer to our sustenance—food and water—and to the dwellings that secure us from the elements and other external dangers. Our need for love is satisfied by parents, guardians, siblings, family, friends, and self. Our need for esteem refers to our position in society and how we feel about ourselves. Self-actualization is the pinnacle we all hope to reach. Explain to the participants that many people cannot communicate effectively because the bottom two needs are not fully met and they may require more effort through communication.

Throughout our lives we work toward self-actualization, which translates into a peaceful, comfortable zone where we know who we are and what we stand for as well as our values and disposition. Most of this self-actualization is realized through our ability to read, talk, discuss, and communicate our thoughts and ideas. However, our success at communication begins when the basic needs of food and shelter are met because they give us the foundation for confidence and development.

9:10   Break (15 minutes)

9:25   Learning review (5 minutes)

Do a quick review of elements studied so far to assess progress and understanding. As you toss a rubber ball to several participants, one after the other, ask the catcher a question about information already covered.

9:30   "You/I" messages (5 minutes)

Show PowerPoint slide 8–10 and pass out Tool 12–6.

Explain the results that will occur when messages contain "you" or "I" in the delivery: "you" points blame; "I" accepts responsibility for an action or feeling. When messages are delivered appropriately, results are positive. Read each example of a "you" message in the slide's left-hand column and then read the "I" message on the right. Point out how the change in pronoun changes the feelings generated by the remark.

9:35   Interpersonal skills (25 minutes)

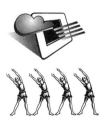

Show PowerPoint slide 8–11 and conduct Learning Activity 10–9.

Explain that this exercise enables a person to step back from subjectivity and look at a situation objectively. Taking the self out of the equation opens a path to resolving a difficult situation. As a group discuss the questions provided for debriefing in the learning activity.

Pass out Tools 12–7 and 12–8 to each class member and review the information contained therein.

Give each participant a copy of Assessment 11–5: Interpersonal Skills. Ask participants to think of a recent meeting they had in the workplace and to answer the questions accordingly. Also advise them that this will be a useful tool in future meetings when they return to their organizations.

10:00   Conflict resolution (10 minutes)

Show PowerPoint slides 8–12 and 8–13 and distribute Tool 12–9. Review and discuss the five elements of conflict resolution on these slides as a way to identify what's required for conflict resolution.

10:10   I Want It! (5 minutes)

Show PowerPoint slide 8–14 and conduct Learning Activity 10–10. This activity reinforces the frustration felt when no headway is made in a communication situation. There is no win–win resolution, only an impasse.

10:15   Ten Questions About Conflict (30 minutes)

Show slide 8–15 and conduct Learning Activity 10–11. The activity will bring the real issues about a specific conflict to the fore because participants are asked to use an actual event in the activity (one that the participant was involved in or learned about in a meeting at his or her workplace). When individual participants have completed their lists of questions, it is helpful to have them discuss the questions in groups of four so that participants are both examining deeply their own conflict situations and giving input about others' situations. Both efforts are learning opportunities. Use the debriefing questions in the learning activity when the groups have finished their work.

10:45 Resolving conflict with difficult personalities (10 minutes)

Show PowerPoint slides 8–16 and 8–17. Review with participants productive behaviors to adopt when dealing with aggressive, undermining, unresponsive, or egoistic people.

10:55 Journaling (5 minutes)

Distribute copies of Tool 12–2: Journal Pages. Ask participants to write what lessons about conflict resolution they have learned in the workshop, and instruct them to relate those specifically to their workplaces.

11:00 Lunch (1 hour)

Noon Learning review (10 minutes)

Toss around the rubber ball again and ask participants questions relating to the first half of the workshop.

Then ask them to change where they are sitting so as to alter the dynamics of the room. Give them a few minutes to get to know the people around them.

12:10 p.m. Persuasion (30 minutes)

Distribute copies of Tool 12–10 and explain the persuasion guidelines.

Conduct Learning Activity 10–12 to give trainees a chance to practice and observe persuasive communication. Show PowerPoint slide 8–18.

Begin by asking for a volunteer to leave the room. Be gentle and careful of feelings toward the person who leaves. Participants who are asked to leave the room can feel nervous about what will happen while they are outside or about their role when they return. It is important for you to ensure that all participants are comfortable at all times. Advise the participant that he or she is playing an important role in the activity and that he or she will not be hurt or embarrassed by the process.

Then show PowerPoint slide 8–19 and ask for a second volunteer who will act as a "persuader." Explain that the persuader's task is to persuade the volunteer outside to hand over an object of some value (for example, a watch, glasses, a pin, a necklace). Turn the slide off and call the first volunteer back into the room.

Give five minutes for the exercise. Then discuss the experience as a class and note on the flipchart which skills cited in Tool 12–10 were effective in the persuasion.

12:40   Using persuasion strategies (30 minutes)

Show slide 8–20 and conduct Learning Activity 10–13. Explain the exercise and point out that participants will use the strategies identified in Tool 12–10 to devise an action plan. The group will form pairs for the first part of the exercise, and then regroup as a class to debrief.

1:10   Journaling (5 minutes)

Refer to Tool 12–2 and have participants continue with the journal they started in the first half of the workshop. Recommend that they transform their discoveries from Learning Activity 10–13 into a specific plan they can execute when they return to the workplace.

1:15   Break (10 minutes)

1:25   Negotiation (35 minutes)

Distribute copies of Tool 12–11 and briefly review the negotiation strategies presented there.

Show PowerPoint slide 8–21 and conduct Learning Activity 10–14.

Ask the participants to form groups of four. Give them 10 minutes to discuss a situation that requires negotiation. Each group should develop a different negotiation situation (for example, negotiating an increase in pay or changing members on a team). In addition, ask them to define a satisfactory outcome from the negotiation. Give each group a flipchart and marking pen and instruct the group to list the requisite steps in the negotiation. After 15 minutes bring the groups back together to debrief.

2:00   Assessing and improving negotiation skills (10 minutes)

Pass out copies of Assessment 11–6 and ask the participants to answer the questions posed there.

2:10   Feedback (45 minutes)

Pass out copies of Tool 12–12 and review the feedback guidelines presented there.

Show PowerPoint slide 8–22. Give each participant a copy of Training Instrument 10–2 and conduct Learning Activity 10–15.

In this activity, ask class members to complete the questionnaire (Training Instrument 10–2). Then have them form groups of four. One participant in each group will question another participant about his or her answer to question 3. The remaining two group members will observe, take notes, and give recommendations at the conclusion of the activity. Allow 20 minutes for this. Reassemble the whole class to discuss the exercise.

2:55   Journaling (5 minutes)

Refer to Tool 12–2 and ask participants to write about their discoveries from this exercise and to set some specific feedback goals for the workplace.

3:00   Stretch break (5 minutes)

3:05   The Johari Window (45 minutes)

Show PowerPoint slide 8–23 and explain how the Johari Window functions and how it can be used to produce effective feedback.

Explain to the participants that the Johari Window exemplifies how we communicate our knowledge of ourselves to others:

♦ Box 1 illustrates the Public Self—the areas of ourselves that we are comfortable sharing with others.

♦ Box 2 identifies the key to feedback through identifi-
cation of our "blind spots." Other people often see
our weaknesses or foibles that are not apparent to us.
When participants learn to receive feedback from
other people, whether positive or negative, accelerat-
ed learning takes place. Because the information is
now available to us, we can work on changes and development within ourselves.

♦ Box 3 contains the information that we hold private
and don't readily share with others. Some participants may prefer not to put any information in this
box because it opens them up more than they may
like. However, when an element of private information is shared with a communication partner or a
group, steps are taken toward a more open and effective communication situation.

♦ Box 4 describes the part of ourselves that we are
"growing into." It is our path toward self-actualization
described in Maslow's Hierarchy of Needs.

In this workshop the Johari Window is being used pri-
marily for Box 2—to identify blind spots in each participant's self-knowledge.

Show PowerPoint slide 8–24. Distribute copies of Training Instrument 10–3 and conduct Learning Activity
10–16.

When forming pairs for the exercise, remember that a
pair that works together on the job will have a better opportunity to make specific feedback recommendations
for each other. With pairs that have not met before the
workshop, ask them to give feedback based on observations from the workshop.

Following the activity, regroup as a whole and ask for
volunteers to share any blind spot that was opened for
them. Handle responses with care and sensitivity because

this is often new information and can make some participants nervous.

3:50   Journaling (5 minutes)

Refer to Tool 12–2 and ask participants to make specific entries about the feedback they have received using the Johari Window.

3:55   Workshop review (30 minutes)

Show PowerPoint slide 8–25. Give pairs of participants 15 minutes to define three key skills that they are taking away from the workshop and that they will apply on the job. Invite all participants to present their three skills to the whole class and to describe how they plan to use them on the job. This process provides a review of the day's learning.

Show PowerPoint slide 8–26 and summarize the topics covered in the workshop.

4:25   Workshop evaluation (10 minutes)

Distribute Assessment 11–7: Course and Facilitator Evaluation and give members of the class 10 minutes to complete it. This enables them to give feedback concerning the facilitator and the workshop.

4:35   Ask for and answer any final questions. Conclude the workshop with handshakes and business card exchanges.

If the organization for which the facilitator is presenting the training requires specific evaluations to be completed, these should be handed out at this point.

What to Do Next

♦ When you are planning your workshop with the organizer, either internally or externally, start identifying dates early (this can sometimes mean six months in advance) and provide several available date options. When more than 10 participants are to attend the workshop, schedules can be challenging to coordinate.

◆　Prepare for the full-day workshop by reviewing the workshop objectives and becoming fully conversant with the content of the slides and other materials. Be sure you are ready to answer questions that arise from group discussions.

◆　Compile the learning activities, handouts, and slides you will use in your training.

◆　Mentally walk through your workshop, hour by hour, checking each training activity to ensure that you have the appropriate materials for each activity.

◆　If the training room is outside your organization, compile a list of questions that you can ask your contact person to determine the room requirements. (Examples of these questions appear in chapter 4.)

◆　Make a checklist of the equipment or classroom tools that you will need to take with you or provide. (See chapter 4 for further details.)

◆　Check the times allotted on your agenda and make yourself a simple timetable to leave prominently displayed on your desk in the training room. For example, if a module is to begin at 9:00 a.m. and end at 9:30 a.m., have this module clearly defined on your timetable.

◆ ◆ ◆

Longer programs offer more possibility for skill development among the participants. If you have the opportunity to provide a two-day workshop, the materials in this chapter can be combined with those in chapter 9.

Slide 8–1

Welcome

to a Full-Day
Effective Communication
Workshop

Name of Organization
Date
Facilitator's Name

Slide 8–2

Agenda

- Welcome and introduction
- Icebreaker activity
- Goal setting
- Communication paradigms
- Maslow's Hierarchy of Needs
- You – I messages
- Interpersonal skills
- Conflict resolution

Slide 8–3

Agenda

- Ten questions about conflict
- Summary of conflict resolution
- Persuasion
- Negotiation
- Feedback
- Johari Window
- Summary and close

Slide 8–4

Class Reunion

Have fun!

Slide 8–5

Goal Setting

- What do you want to learn today?

- What tools do you want to take back to the workplace?

- What do you need to help you improve?

Use your journal to capture these thoughts.

Slide 8–6

Participant Introductions

- Form pairs.

- Exchange the following information:
  - Where were you born and raised?
  - What's your favorite food?
  - What are your goals for this workshop?

- Introduce your partner to the whole class and include your partner's goals.

Slide 8–7

Communication Paradigms

- Know your frame of reference.
- Why is the information being exchanged?
- What does the recipient need from you?
- What do you need from the recipient?

To be effective we should diagnose before we prescribe.

Slide 8–8

Communication Paradigms

- Will the information affect status?
- Is the organizational hierarchy in play?
- Is the information being received through a confrontational filter?
- Is everyone on the same map?

Slide 8–9

Maslow's Hierarchy of Needs

➤ Individuals strive to satisfy five basic needs.

➤ Needs are hierarchical.

➤ When a need is satisfied, it no longer motivates an individual.

Slide 8–10

You Messages and I Messages

"You" Message	*"I" Message*
• You really wrecked the project when you took over.	• I feel very upset about the direction the project has taken since you took over.
• I can't believe you did that.	• I am really upset about the decision you made.
• You don't even care about the success of this project.	• I feel disappointed because it seems you're not concerned about the success of the project.

Slide 8–11

Depersonalizing the Personal

➤ Form groups of four people.
➤ Think of a challenging situation.
➤ Describe your situation, omitting personal pronouns (I, me, my, mine, and so forth).
➤ Select a spokesperson from your group to report to the whole group.

Slide 8–12

Conflict Resolution

Four Steps to Resolution:

- Define: the problem
- Clarify: key players and expectations
- Identify: action steps for resolution
- Resolve: by taking the steps

Slide 8–13

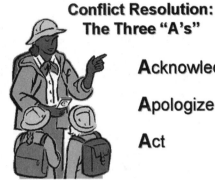

Conflict Resolution: The Three "A's"

Acknowledge

Apologize

Act

Slide 8–14

I Want It!

➢ Find a partner.
➢ One member of the pair possesses an unnamed object that the other person wants.
➢ The dialogue for the owner is only _You can't have it!_
➢ The dialogue for the other is only _I want it!_
➢ Take two minutes for this exercise, including a role swap. It will get noisy!
➢ Regroup and report on the frustrations

Slide 8–15

Ten Questions About Conflict

- Think about a current or past professional conflict.
- Write 10 questions for the people involved in the conflict.
- If time permits, write 10 questions that others in the conflict may have for you.
- Debrief as a whole group.

Slide 8–16

Conflict Resolution: Reacting to Difficult Personalities

- **Aggressive:** Listen carefully. Avoid arguing. Be formal. Use the person's name. Be clear with your responses.

- **Undermining:** Focus on the issues and don't acknowledge sarcasm. Don't overreact.

Slide 8–17

Reacting to Difficult Personalities

- **Unresponsive:** Ask open-ended questions. Be silent and wait for responses. Be patient and positive.

- **Egoist:** Make sure you know the facts. Agree when possible. Ask questions and listen. Disagree only when you _know_ you are right.

Slide 8–18

Persuasion Exercise

- Ask a volunteer to leave the room.

- Ask another volunteer to be the "persuader."

Slide 8–19

Persuasion Exercise

- The persuader's goal is to get an object (for example, watch, pin, tie) from the person outside the room when he or she returns.

- Call the outside volunteer back into the room and take five minutes for the exercise.

- Debrief as a group, discussing the verbal and body language used.

<u>Facilitator:</u> **Remove this slide when the outside volunteer returns to the room.**

Slide 8–20

Persuasion Strategies

- Write brief details of a professional situation that will require persuasion (for example, new policy, team changes).

- Additionally, write brief details of the characteristics of the people who must be persuaded (for example, stubborn, sensitive, resistant to change).

- Form pairs and help one another devise a plan for successful persuasion.

- Debrief with the whole class.

Use your journal to capture the strategies.

Slide 8–21

Negotiation Exercise

- Form groups of four people each and get a flipchart and pen for each group.

- Take 10 minutes to formulate a negotiation situation.

- Define a satisfactory outcome from the negotiation.

- Take 30 minutes to discuss and record the requisite steps for success.

- Choose a spokesperson for your group.

- Gather with the whole class to debrief. Spokespeople present their groups' plans.

- Role-play one of the plans.

Slide 8–22

Feedback Exercise

- Complete the questionnaire.

- Form groups of four people.

- One participant will be "interviewed" by another in the group about his or her answer to question 3.

- Two participants will observe, take notes, and give recommendations at the conclusion of the activity.

- Take 30 minutes for this exercise.

- Debrief as a whole group.

Use your journal to capture tools.

Slide 8–23

The Johari Window
(Developed by Joseph Luft and Harrington Ingham)

1. I know Others know **Open/Public Self**	2. I don't know Others know **Blind Spot**
3. I know Others don't know **Private Self**	4. I don't know Others don't know **Unknown Self**

Slide 8–24

Johari Window Exercise

➢ Form pairs. (If members of a pair work together at the same organization, they will have specific areas for feedback. Those who don't work together may give feedback based on observations from the workshop.)

➢ Focus on box 2 of the Johari Window (the blind spot).

➢ Each person in the pair gives feedback to the other person on his or her blind spot.

➢ Allow 15 minutes for the exercise.

➢ Regroup to debrief. One volunteer can share his or her blind-spot discovery.

Use your journal to capture these discoveries.

Slide 8–25

Workshop Review

- With a partner, define three key skills that each person is taking away from the workshop.

- Take three minutes to describe your skills to the class.

Slide 8–26

Summary and Close

- Personal goal setting
- Communication paradigms
- Maslow's Hierarchy
- You – I messages
- Interpersonal skills
- Conflict resolution

- Ten questions about conflict
- Summary of conflict resolution
- Persuasion
- Negotiation
- Feedback
- Johari Window

Two-Day Communication Skills Workshop

What's in This Chapter

- Objectives for the two-day communication skills workshop
- List of materials for the facilitator and the participants
- Sample program agenda

An extended workshop offers a venue for more comprehensive instruction, increased time to spend on the learning activities, and greater opportunity to practice the skills being taught. In some instances you can enroll a larger number of participants in an extended workshop because they can be broken up into pairs or small groups for study, investigation, and practice. In a two-day workshop there is a greater opportunity for participants to explore the learning because of the additional day. Even though participants work in pairs or small groups in shorter programs too, in a two-day program they can perform self-guided work and can coach each other. In the longer workshop, participants get to know each other and become familiar with each other's learning styles. Partnerships frequently form and that enhances the communication in the workshop and in the workplace.

When participants are required to explore in-depth communication skills because there are communication challenges within their organization, a two-day workshop allows this exploration to take place at a deeper level. On the first day, participants get to know each other and begin to learn each other's styles and methods of communication. On the second day, barriers frequently drop away and that enables improved collaboration and discussion.

The learning elements included in the one-day seminar will apply in the longer program, but the time allotted for each one can be extended.

As the facilitator, you may want to work with flipchart pages hung on your office wall as you begin to shape the second day using the material given in this chapter. Outlining the topics you're going to present on large sheets of paper lets you see the training day taking shape and lets you add your own ideas to make the workshop more personal and even more compelling.

You might use a video camera during a longer workshop to record and review progress and development, especially in public speaking activities. Then you can ask participants to review the video in pairs away from the main workshop room while you teach other elements. **Note:** If participants are going to be absent from the training room while new material is being covered, you need to clarify with the hiring organization which elements of the training are required for all participants in the workshop. If the organization commits to a one-day training and wishes the participants to learn presentation skills with videotaping, then you must be flexible and determine which learning modules can be omitted from the workshop to accommodate the presentation skills training.

You may wish to provide a theme for the longer workshop—something that can become a central learning focus. For example, consider "Communication Is the Key." You can earmark each learning activity with a picture of a key to focus attention on the specifics required for that module. You might include class competitions to see which participant can unlock the most clues in the shortest time. Be creative in devising your theme, and stick with it to tie all of the elements of the learning together and make the experience more memorable.

Guest speakers are an excellent resource for a longer workshop. A change of face and pace for the participants is an energizing boost. Be sure you know the speaker's style and skills before he or she takes part in your workshop. Also be sure to make it clear to the guest how much time he or she will have to speak, and enforce that limit gently if needed.

Quizzes are a fun way to review learning and invigorate learners in a longer workshop. We all reach a heightened sense of awareness before an examination so including quizzes throughout the workshop will keep participants on their toes.

Two-day programs can be held on consecutive days or as much as a week apart. Separating sessions by more than a week lets participants lose momentum.

When a two-day workshop is spread across two weeks, a review of the first session at the beginning of the second session is vital. In a longer workshop, participants may be invited to present portions of the curriculum for the whole class. Participants enjoy a change of facilitator, and it gives you the chance to assess the material you've presented from an objective standpoint. Have you been succinct? Are your teaching methods clear and accessible? Are the participants understanding what you're teaching them and assimilating the skills?

When the sessions are a week apart, homework may be set to keep the participants connected to the workshop. Do refrain from giving hours of homework, however, because most class members will be returning to the workforce and will have their own professional and personal lives to manage. In a communication workshop, a very useful homework assignment is to ask participants to observe, practice, and make notes of communication in their workplaces. They will gain interesting insights while putting their own learning into practice. In addition, you might ask them to develop case studies from their observations.

Occasionally it's important that you have some contact with the participants between sessions to review their off-site progress or simply to stay connected.

Extended programs are not without possible problems. For example, if there is friction between two participants on the first day of the workshop, the chances are it will increase over a longer period. As the facilitator you'll need to contain negativity and avoid conflicts that derail the learning for everyone in the room. You must be skilled in relationship building as well as communication.

A two-day workshop can be tiring for you and for the participants. Therefore, periods of quiet time, longer breaks, and energizers throughout are important additions.

In the end, how you design and implement your two-day workshop is your choice, but remember that the participants are your focus and their needs must be met. Including some of the above elements and being prepared to counteract possible problems will ensure an open, progressive learning environment and meaningful results.

So let's prepare an agenda for the extended workshop. In this chapter we'll explore the second half of the two-day workshop. For a two-day program, the materials and activities covered in chapter 8 of this workbook form the first day. Simply replace the Welcome, Agenda, and Summary and Close slides in the *One-Day.ppt* presentation with the Welcome, Agenda, and Summary and Close slides from the *Two-Day.ppt* presentation.

Objectives of the Two-Day Session

The participants' objectives in the second day of a two-day session are to

- ♦ understand the differences between aggressiveness and assertiveness

- ♦ study and employ professional language skills

- ♦ design and develop a three-key-point presentation

- ♦ practice effective public speaking skills

- ♦ develop stories and analogies to include in a public speech

- ♦ study the strategies for successful meetings.

Materials

There are a number of things you will need to put together to be prepared to facilitate the workshop. The list below will help you prepare properly.

For the facilitator:

- ♦ Projector, screen, and computer for running the PowerPoint presentation

- ♦ PowerPoint slides 9–1 through 9–21 (*Two-Day.ppt* on the CD)

- ♦ Learning Activity 10–8: Icebreaker: Class Reunion

- ♦ Learning Activity 10–17: Assertiveness—Making Your Case

- ♦ Learning Activity 10–18: Vocal Exercises

- ♦ Learning Activity 10–19: Storytelling

- ♦ Learning Activity 10–20: Analogies

- ♦ Assessment 11–1: Client Survey and Needs Analysis (distributed one month before the workshop begins)

- ♦ Rubber ball

- ◆ Flipchart and marking pen

- ◆ 3 x 5-inch note cards

- ◆ Video camera with tripod

- ◆ VCR player and viewing monitor

- ◆ Extra room for videotape reviews

For the participants:

- ◆ Copies of PowerPoint slides 9–1 through 9–21 to be used as a workshop handout. Black-and-white versions of the slides can be printed from the overhead masters file, *Two-Day.pps,* on the CD. (We suggest that you print three slides per page.)

- ◆ Tool 12–1: Frequently Used Action Verbs

- ◆ Tool 12–2: Journal Pages

- ◆ Tool 12–13: Conflict in Team Meetings

- ◆ Tool 12–14: Fun Phrases and Tongue Twisters (optional)

- ◆ Tool 12–15: Delivery Skills for Effective Presentations

- ◆ Tool 12–16: What Influences an Audience

- ◆ Tool 12–17: Steps for Developing a Three-Point Presentation

- ◆ Tool 12–18: All About Storytelling

- ◆ Tool 12–19: Using Stories and Analogies

- • Tool 12–20: Strategies for Effective Meetings

- ◆ Training Instrument 9–1: Evaluation of a Presentation

- ◆ Assessment 11–7: Course and Facilitator Evaluation

- ◆ One blank videotape for each participant

- ◆ Flipchart and marking pen (one set for each group of four participants)

- ◆ Toys such as squeeze balls, Lego® blocks, pipe cleaners, or Play-Doh®. (Some people like to keep their hands busy because it helps them focus their listening, and these toys give them the opportunity to do so. It's like doodling [scribbling], which many people do while a facilitator is teaching. It keeps the brainwaves open during the learning process. Kinesthetic learners typically prefer something to manipulate while they participate in learning.)

Using the CD

Materials for this training session are provided in this workbook and as electronic files on the accompanying CD. To access the electronic files, insert the CD and click on the appropriate Adobe .pdf documents. Further directions and help using the files can be found in the appendix, "Using the Compact Disc," at the back of this workbook.

It's important that you review all of the slides as part of your preparation for the workshop. At that time you should plan explanations and examples for concepts presented in the slides.

Sample Agenda

The times assigned to the elements of this training are approximate and will vary with discussion and facilitator emphasis.

Note: Remember that we're covering only the second day in this agenda. For the first day of a two-day program, refer to chapter 8.

8:00 a.m.   Welcome and introduction (5 minutes)

Show PowerPoint slides 9–1 and 9–2. You will already know the participants; however, be sure to make them feel just as welcome as you did on Day One.

8:05   Topic and skills review (10 minutes)

Review the topics and skills learned on Day One, using the rubber ball tossed to participants, one by one, to check that they have retained what was covered. Also seek any questions still remaining from Day One.

8:15   Icebreaker: Learning Activity 10–8 (5 minutes)

Expect and encourage plenty of noise and energy as the participants greet each other again.

8:20   Assertiveness vs. aggressiveness (30 minutes)

Show PowerPoint slide 9–3. Delineate the subtle differences between assertion and aggression. Discuss how assertion is a positive approach to making a point, whereas aggression tends to be a negative or harsh approach. The main point is that effective communication requires that aggression be replaced with assertiveness.

Pass out copies of Tool 12–13 and conduct Learning Activity 10–17. Guide the participants through a reading of the case study in Tool 12–13. Have the class form groups of four and supply each group with a flipchart and marking pen. Direct the groups to rewrite the scenario, replacing aggressive language with assertive language. Ask them to write their final versions on their flipcharts.

Regroup as a whole to debrief the exercise, using the discussion questions at the end of the learning activity.

8:50   Use of voice and language (30 minutes)

Show PowerPoint slide 9–4. Explain that one's voice is one's logo—it expresses what he or she knows and feels and who he or she is. It is the indicator of mood, of confidence, and of state of mind. A dull monotone will put an audience to sleep so effective communication demands that the voice be well-articulated (that is, mouth is open and words are pronounced clearly), modulated (that is, voice level fluctuates up and down), and set at a good pace. The average listener (audience member) is approximately 10 to 15 words behind the speaker in assimilating the message, and the speaker must insert pauses so that the audience can catch up and do the mental work required to understand the message.

Show PowerPoint slide 9–5, which refers to vocal emphasis. The main point concerns the delivery style of the message. Dr. Albert Mehrabian discovered in his surveys that nearly 40 percent of the ease of receiving a spoken message is in the way it is delivered. If the message is positive and uplifting, the speaker should be appropriately

animated, smiling, and putting vigor into the words. When the occasion is serious or of vital importance to the listeners, the words should be conveyed with a suitable solemnity (not the same as a deadly monotone) and with a measured pace.

In our busy world, simple is best. As a facilitator you are more effective when you use words like "get" rather than "retrieve," or "look at" rather than "investigate." This is especially important when you have participants from diverse cultural backgrounds and with different native languages in your workshop. Make your language accessible and easy for them.

As a facilitator in communication, you set an example with your speech and especially your grammar. Therefore it is important that you use correct grammar. You do not, however, have a right to correct a participant's grammar unless he or she specifically asks you to do so. If necessary, refer participants to one of the grammar books listed in the "For Further Reading" section at the back of this workbook.

Jargon, slang, and acronyms are useful in everyday communication inside organizations because they speed up the process if everyone understands them. In a workshop, however, not everyone shares or understands the same terminology. Use straightforward and understandable language.

Show PowerPoint slide 9–6. Distribute copies of Tool 12–14 (if you have decided to include this variation) and Tool 12–1.

Conduct Learning Activity 10–18: Vocal Exercises. Lead the participants in the breathing and relaxation exercises, followed by the optional fun phrases and tongue twisters (PowerPoint slides 9–7 and 9–8). These activities relax the participants and improve and project their voices.

Follow the exercises in the learning activity with the list of Frequently Used Action Verbs in Tool 12–1. Ask the participants to form groups of four in which each participant will select four words, one from each column (for example, *authorize, distribute, monitor, review*). Taking turns, each group member will make four strong, directive statements using one of the chosen words in each statement to practice the use of their exercised voices.

9:20 Journaling (5 minutes)

Pass out copies of Tool 12–2. Ask participants to write about what they have learned thus far in today's session.

9:25 Break (15 minutes)

9:40 Skills for effective presentations (20 minutes)

Note: The activities used to train participants on presentation skills will take about two morning hours. You may have to adjust your lunch time, depending on the number of participants in the workshop.

Show PowerPoint slide 9–9 and distribute Tool 12–15. Explain the five pointers listed on the slide:

1. Confident body language is very important for successful presentations. Ask participants to stand and place their weight firmly on the balls of their feet and to imagine a string that runs from the top of their head to the ceiling. This will help give them a posture that conveys confidence and poise.

2. Explain that eye *contact* is a glance at an audience member, but eye *connection* lasts for three to five seconds per audience member and is very useful for slowing down a speaker's fast pace and for giving individual audience members the impression that the speaker is addressing them only.

3. A speaker's movements must be smooth and have a purpose. Explain to participants that the speaker must walk slowly toward an audience member while addressing that person. Then the speaker could stop, add additional message points, and move in another direc-

tion, connecting with an audience members in that direction.

4. Although we use gestures nearly all the time in conversation, participants may struggle with gestures while speaking to an audience. Explain that a presentation is really a conversation and that participants should use their normal gestures. Ask them to begin with their hands at waist level in a lightly clasped position, then open the palms and speak with emphasis, using strong hand gestures to underline points. The bigger the gesture, the more confident the speaker looks, and he or she will convey that to the audience, which in turn will feel confident.

5. Remind participants to do a few vocal exercises before they begin their presentations so that the voice is strong and projects to the last row of listeners.

In general, to feel confident in front of an audience, participants must understand that the process is about (and for) the audience, not about (and for) the speaker. To convey the message effectively, the participant must make eye connection with listeners and focus only on them from the beginning. Using strong and open gestures releases nervous energy and helps build confidence. When audience members feel the confidence transmitted from a speaker and know that the presentation is for them, they relax and give a positive response to the speaker. A win–win situation is the result.

Turn to Tool 12–15 and cover the additional information it contains. Give trainees the chance to practice these skills by giving a one-minute speech on a simple topic. Show PowerPoint slide 9–10 to suggest topics.

10:00   What influences an audience (10 minutes)

Show PowerPoint slide 9–11 and distribute copies of Tool 12–16: What Influences an Audience.

Emphasize the point that a speech is "about" the audience by explaining what factors influence an audience.

We cannot (ostensibly) change the first three—race, gender, and age. Therefore, when a participant is a young female addressing a group of middle-aged men, her impact may not be strong because the group may prefer a middle-aged (white) male to speak to them. But when the young female ensures that the last four elements are practiced, she will gain confidence in front of this particular audience.

Explain that the filling of personal space goes hand in hand with confidence and posture. Advise the participants to take ownership of the front of the room when they are speaking and, in filling the space, to increase their authority.

Stress the importance of speaking with energy or with passion. This means getting the whole body involved in the delivery. When the speaker is passionate about his or her topic, it's easy for the audience to become fully engaged.

Although the handshake is presented last on this slide, it is important for the participants to understand that at the outset of a presentation there is power and connection in a firm handshake. We recommend that participants shake hands with as many audience members as possible *before they speak* because it provides an icebreaker and creates a sense of community in the room.

10:10   Developing a three-point presentation (10 minutes)

Show PowerPoint slides 9–12 and distribute copies of Tool 12–17: Steps for Developing a Three-Point Presentation.

Studies have shown that an audience can easily absorb three key message points. If the speaker goes beyond three points, however, the listeners' attention spans wane, absorption rates begin to slow, and their focus will drift. We recommend three key points because it is normally possible for the speaker to recall this number of points without using notes. (Remember, of course, that slides serve effectively as speaker notes if needed.) Think of the three-point presentation as a triangle—one of the most enduring geometrical patterns in history—and you'll know you're creating a solid speaking foundation.

Show PowerPoint slide 9–13. Review the additional guidance for making effective presentations.

10:20   Preparing a presentation (20 minutes)

Show PowerPoint slide 9–14. Ask participants to form pairs and give them 10 minutes to help each other create an outline for a professional speech, using the guidelines presented on the slide.

Bring pairs into groups of four and ask each participant to deliver his or her outline to the group. Instruct the listeners to evaluate the outline on the basis of message clarity.

10:40   Learning about stories and analogies (15 minutes)

Distribute copies of Tool 12–18: All About Storytelling. Explain that a story is a personal experience that can vividly illustrate a point in a presentation. Audiences love stories and our lives are full of them, but we don't always know how to deliver them effectively. Review with participants the guidance given in the tool so they can understand and experience successful storytelling.

Tell your own story to help the participants understand the process.

Now distribute copies of Tool 12–19: Using Stories and Analogies. Explain that an analogy is a parallel to a real-life situation and it frequently helps an audience understand something complex or something ordinarily outside their reach. Review the information on the tool with the participants.

10:55   Telling a story (30 minutes)

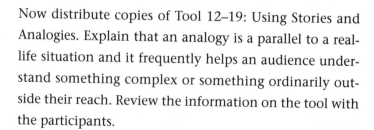

Show PowerPoint slide 9–15. Ask participants to form groups of four and undertake the exercise in Learning Activity 10–19. During this period each group member will have up to three minutes to tell his or her story to the

others in the group. After each story, the listeners will briefly retell the outline of the story to the speaker to ensure that they have understood it. Ask them to advise the speaker about the story's appropriateness for the presentation. Discuss the exercise as a whole group.

11:25   Devising analogies (20 minutes)

Show PowerPoint slide 9–16. Divide participants into two groups and give each group a flipchart and marking pen. Conduct Learning Activity 10–20, in which the groups will develop as many analogies as they can in five minutes. **Note:** Making this a competition between the two groups increases people's energy and attention. You might want to give a small prize to the winning group.

Discuss this activity as a whole group. Then give participants five minutes to decide if and where an analogy or analogies will fit into the presentations they are planning.

Ask each person to return to the partner with whom he or she was working before the analogy exercise. Give them time to discuss and identify the appropriate place for a story or analogy in their presentations.

11:45   Lunch (1 hour)

12:45 p.m.   Delivering and videotaping presentations (90 minutes)

Ask each participant to deliver his or her presentation (up to five minutes in length) to the rest of the class. Videotape each presentation. When two participants have delivered their presentations, give each a copy of Training Instrument 9–1: Evaluation of a Presentation and direct them to an adjoining room where they can view the videos and evaluate each presentation. Repeat this for every two participants until everyone has had an opportunity to present and to complete the evaluation.

2:15   Giving feedback (30 minutes)

When each participant has reviewed his or her video and that of his or her partner, invite people to give the class one-minute summaries of the partner's presenting skills.

2:45   Journaling (5 minutes)

Pass out copies of Tool 12–2 and ask participants to write about the lessons they learned in creating, giving, viewing, and evaluating the presentations.

2:50   Break (10 minutes)

3:00   Strategies for successful meetings (1 hour)

Show PowerPoint slides 9–17 through 9–20. The information on the slides is self-explanatory so ask participants to read it for themselves.

Ask the participants to form groups of four. Distribute copies of Tool 12–20: Strategies for Effective Meetings and have each participant select 1 of the 17 strategic elements presented there. Give them 10 minutes to develop three key points for that element. Then give each person three minutes to present their points to the others in their group.

This activity not only provides a lesson in how to run a successful meeting; it also continues practice with presentations.

4:00   Journaling (5 minutes)

Refer to Tool 12–2 and ask participants to journal what they've learned about conducting effective meetings.

4:05   Summary and close (25 minutes)

Show PowerPoint slide 9–21 and summarize the topics covered on this second day of the workshop. Review the participants' goals from the flipchart. Answer any questions or concerns that arise.

Distribute Assessment 11–7: Course and Facilitator Evaluation and give members of the class 10 minutes to complete it.

Ask for any final comments and contributions, and answer any last questions. Conclude the workshop with handshakes and the exchange of business cards.

Note: In some instances, the organization for which you are facilitating this workshop will require that the participants be evaluated. This is something you will complete in the week (or sooner, depending on the organization's deadline) following the workshop.

What to Do Next

- ◆ Determine the schedule for training classes, reserve location, and identify and invite participants.

- ◆ Ensure you have a second training room available for the reviewing of videotapes by the participants.

- ◆ Double-check to see if you are required to provide a video camera, tripod, and videotapes, or if these will be provided by the hiring organization?

- ◆ Review the workshop objectives and become fully conversant with the content of the slides and other materials. Be sure you are ready to answer questions that arise from group discussions.

- ◆ Compile the learning activities, handouts, and slides you will use in your training.

- ◆ Prepare yourself emotionally and physically for the two-day workshop. Look at your calendar in advance of the workshop and clear or move any stress-related activities so that you can embark on the training with a clear head. Plan to get a good night's rest before the first day and at the end of the second day. (If you are training off-site and the participants want you to have dinner with them, respectfully decline because you won't get a break from teaching if you join them.)

◆ ◆ ◆

Now it's time to move to chapter 10, which contains the learning activities presented in the workshop agendas. You may already have been reviewing them as you read through the planning and execution chapters of this book. Each activity is broken into sections: the objective of the activity; the materials and the time required; your specific preparations for the activity, if any; detailed instructions for conducting the activity; and questions for debriefing with the participants.

Training Instrument 9–1
Evaluation of a Presentation

Instructions: When you have viewed the videotape of your partner's presentation, use this instrument to record your evaluation of that presentation. You will use these notes in class to present a brief assessment of the positive aspects of your partner's work.

Name_____ **Organization**_____

Speech topic: _____

What worked:

Recommendations for the next speech:

Overall observations:

Evaluator's name_____ **Date**_____

Slide 9–1

Welcome

to a Two-Day Effective Communication Workshop

Name of Organization
Date
Facilitator's Name

Slide 9–2

Agenda

- Review of Workshop Day One
- Assertiveness vs. aggression
- Use of voice and language
- Presentation skills
- Storytelling and analogies
- Successful meetings
- Summary and close

Slide 9–3

Assertiveness vs. Aggression

- Assertiveness is positive; aggression is negative.
- Assertiveness conveys influence; aggression displays anger.
- Assertiveness allows progress and direction; aggression creates hostility and roadblocks.

Slide 9–4

Use of Voice and Language

- "Speech is the mirror of the soul" (Socrates).
- Vocal energy is vital for engaging an audience.
- Audiences absorb a message 10 – 15 words behind the speaker's delivery.
- A pause provides a powerful point in a presentation.

Slide 9–5

Vocal Emphasis

- Consider this: It's not what you say; it's how you say it.
- Use simple language.
- Watch your grammar.
- Avoid jargon, slang, and acronyms.
- Remember that 40 percent of the success of communication is in the oral delivery.

Slide 9–6

Exercises for Excellence

- Strengthen your voice.
- Exercise your vocal cords.
- Learn to breathe.
- Relax your body.

Slide 9–7

Fun Phrases

- Billy Button bought a buttered biscuit
- The painted pomp of pleasure's proud parade
- Like clocks, like locks
- Drowsy tinklings lull the distant folds
- Red leather, yellow leather
- A library literally littered with contemporary literature
- Katy caught a naughty kitten
- Helen heard the horses' hooves from her home on the hill
- Last night the cows prowled around the yard
- Dance past the last barn
- Park your car in Harvard yard

Slide 9–8

Tongue Twisters

- Proper copper coffee pot
- Mixed biscuits
- Six thistles
- Cup of cocoa
- Little kettles
- Purple metal
- Lovely yellow lilies
- Singing kettles
- Tipping teapots
- The Leith police dismisseth us

Slide 9–9

How to Deliver Effective Presentations

- Pay attention to posture and poise.
- Maintain eye connection.
- Use fluid movements.
- Make expressive gestures.
- Project your voice.

Successful presentations are not about the speaker; they are about the audience.

Slide 9–10

Speech Topics for Practice

- My first or most unusual job
- My favorite sport or hobby
- An object on my desk or in my home
- My favorite book or movie
- What I would do with $1 million

Slide 9–11

What Influences an Audience

- Race
- Gender
- Age
- Posture / confidence / space
- Eye contact / facial expression / energy
- Appearance
- Handshake

"Sometimes, who you are speaks so loudly,
I cannot hear what you are saying."
– Anonymous

Slide 9–12

How to Develop a Three-Point Presentation

- Select a topic.
- Define the objective.
- Develop three key points.
- Add two to three subpoints.
- Create a dynamic opening and closing.

Less is more when creating a successful presentation.

Slide 9–13

More Tools for Presentations

- Research your audience. What do they need to know? What's In It for Them? (WIIFT?)
- Develop your speech *first*, then add your visuals.
- Design appropriate visuals. PowerPoint does not have to be the first choice.
- Rehearse, rehearse, rehearse.
- Put your outline on 3 x 5-inch note cards.
- Don't read your speech. Be "free" for your audience.

Slide 9–14

Guide for Presentations

- Topic
- Objective: To...(persuade, convince, and so forth)
- Define opening
- First key point
  – Sub points
- Second key point
  – Sub points
- Third key point
  – Sub points
- Define close

Slide 9–15

Stories for Presentations

- Think of some task that is part of your job or part of a hobby.
- Take five minutes to write details of a story that explains the task.
- Form groups of four people.
- Choose one person in your group who will take three minutes and tell his or her story to the other three.
- If you were a listener, tell the details back to the storyteller to confirm whether you understood the concepts described.

Slide 9–16

Analogies

- Separate into two groups.
- Get a flipchart and a pen, and select a "scribe" for your group.
- Take 5 minutes as a group to develop as many analogies as you can. Write them on the flipchart.
- Regroup as a whole class and share your lists.
- The facilitator will award prizes to the group with the most analogies.
- For your own use, write down the analogies each group developed.

Slide 9–17

Strategies for Successful Meetings

➢ To meet or not to meet?
- Call a meeting for the right reasons.
- Select attendees with care.
- Create a culture where it is OK not to attend.

➢ Develop an agenda.
- Start with the most important topic.
- Identify discussion points vs. FYI.
- Send agenda and reading materials before the meeting.

Slide 9–18

Strategies for Successful Meetings

➢ Appoint a facilitator and timekeeper.
➢ Create a "parking lot."
➢ Call for a process check regularly.
➢ Leave when you're done.
➢ Serve food.
➢ Allow stretch breaks.
➢ Let participants drive the agenda.
➢ Meet outdoors, or outside the work environment.
➢ Model good meeting behavior.

Slide 9–19

How to Run a Successful Meeting

- Listen to everyone.
- Give others' ideas precedence over yours.
- Assume that everyone's ideas have value.
- Paraphrase, but don't judge.
- Control the dominant people without alienating them.

The answer is in the room. — John Marcus

Slide 9–20

How to Run a Successful Meeting

- Remember that your interest and alertness are contagious.
- Keep track of the agenda and advise the attendees.
- Check with anyone who owns a problem under discussion to find out if it is worth pursuing.
- Ask others to run the meeting. Those who lead, learn.

Filling our ears with all we have learned to say,
we are deaf to what we have to hear.
— Wendell Johnson

Slide 9–21

Summary and Close

- Reviewed Workshop Day One
- Assertiveness vs. aggression
- Use of language
- Presentation skills
- Storytelling and analogies
- Successful meetings
- Review of participants' goals
- Summary and Close

Learning Activities

- Twenty learning activities for use in the workshop sessions

- Complete step-by-step instructions for conducting the learning activities

- Three instruments to cover specific training points

Adult participants enjoy learning activities scattered throughout the content in a workshop. Exercises enliven and invigorate the experience, and they help the learning "stick." The following 20 learning activities provide you with a variety of experiences to offer to your participants in support of the topics covered in the communication skills workshops.

We have allotted a specific amount of time for each activity, but you may change the duration of any activity to fit the number of participants in your workshop or to supply their specific requirements. To fit the topic you're teaching, feel free to customize any of the activities by changing the questions or the materials used in the activity.

Learning Activity 10–1: Icebreaker: Getting to Know You

OBJECTIVES

The objectives of this learning activity are to break the ice and help participants get to know each other before the workshop begins.

MATERIALS

◆ None

TIME

◆ 15 minutes

INSTRUCTIONS

1. Explain that this is an icebreaking activity.

2. Ask participants to stand, move around the room, and shake hands with everyone present (including you).

3. When they have circulated through the whole room, ask each person to select a partner (someone they don't know or someone from another company if the class is mixed).

4. Tell them to exchange three questions:

   ◆ Where were you born and raised?

   ◆ What is your professional role and how did you get into it?

   ◆ What do you want out of this class?

5. Ask pairs of participants to introduce each other to the whole group, using the information their questions have elicited.

6. Debrief, using the discussion questions below.

VARIATION

Vary the questions that the participants ask each other according to the specific goals of the workshop.

DISCUSSION QUESTIONS FOR DEBRIEFING

1. Did you find common ground with the questions?

2. Do you feel more connected to the workshop process?

3. Were there any surprises?

Learning Activity 10–2: Understanding Yourself

OBJECTIVE

The objective of this learning activity is to guide participants through a self-awareness/exploration activity to help them discover how their life experiences influence every communication situation they face.

MATERIALS

◆ Training Instrument 10–1: Circle of Influence

TIME

◆ 15– minutes

PREPARATION

Prepare a copy of Training Instrument 10–1 for each participant.

INSTRUCTIONS

1. Explain that participants will now be asked to reflect on the influences in their lives that have made them who they are today. The main point of this exercise is to make clear that we all view life through the filter of our own experiences.

2. Take a moment to speak personally about the major influences in your life. You are doing this to model the process for your trainees.

3. Pass out copies of Training Instrument 10–1.

4. Describe the drawing as an individual's "circle of influence." The center circle is "you" and the surrounding circles are the influential life experiences (for example, education, family, religion, region, and the like).

5. Ask each trainee to fill in the drawing to reflect his or her own life.

6. When the participants have completed their diagrams, ask them to form pairs and share what they are comfortable sharing with their partners.

7. Debrief, using the discussion questions below.

Training Instrument 10–1
The Circle of Influence

Instructions: Place yourself in the large circle in the center. In the surrounding smaller circles, list the major influences that make you the person you are.

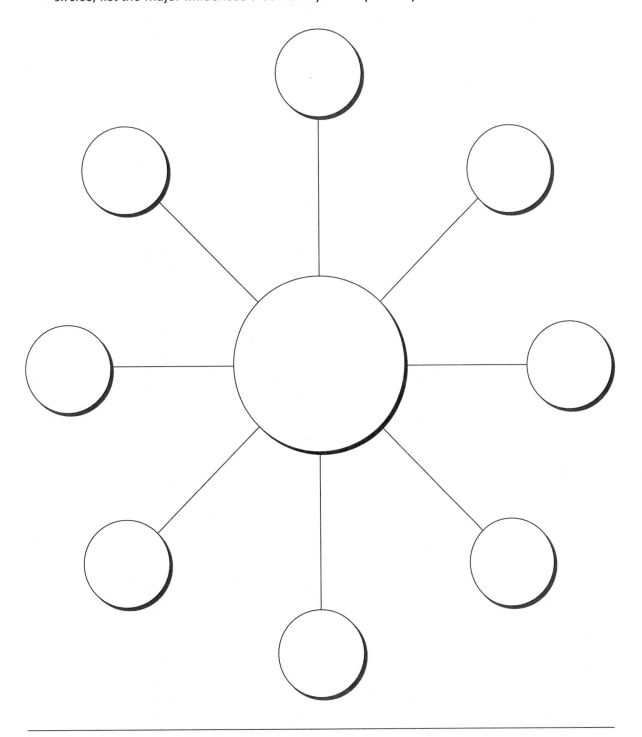

DISCUSSION QUESTIONS FOR DEBRIEFING

1.   What are your thoughts about this exercise?

2.   Oftentimes, when we meet people we realize pretty quickly that either we like them or we don't. Why do you think that's so?

3.   How often do you "clean your filter"?

Learning Activity 10–3:
Icebreaker: Life Is Just a Bowl of Candies

OBJECTIVE

The objective of this learning activity is to help participants learn more about each other.

MATERIALS

- ◆ A variety of wrapped candies (remember to avoid candies with nuts and to include some sugar-free candies)

- ◆ A bowl or basket for the candies

TIME

- ◆ 10 minutes

INSTRUCTIONS

1. Offer participants a bowl of candies as they first enter the classroom. Ask each person to take as many as he or she would like.

2. When all trainees are seated, have each of them count the number of candies he or she has.

3. Beginning at a point of your choice in the room, ask each participant to tell the group one fact about himself or herself for every piece of candy taken. This can create humor if a person has taken more than 10 candies and is required to "stretch" some of the facts.

4. Debrief, using the discussion questions below.

DISCUSSION QUESTIONS FOR DEBRIEFING

1. How did you feel when you were asked to take the candies?

2. How did you feel about the number of candies you took?

3. Was it more fun to share your facts or listen to others?

Learning Activity 10–4: The Listening Stick

OBJECTIVE

The objective of this learning activity is to enable participants to experience one level of listening.

MATERIALS

- ◆ A time-keeping device (for example, a watch, stopwatch, egg timer)
- ◆ Pen or pencil for each student to use as a listening stick

TIME

- ◆ 10–15 minutes

INSTRUCTIONS

1. In this activity, an item to hold is used as a reminder to listeners to focus on the speaker, not on oneself or on what the listener will get to say next. Explain that this practice comes from Native American culture where the item used is a beautifully decorated stick of some sort. The stick has also been referred to as a talking stick, meaning that when you are holding the stick it is your turn to talk.

2. Instruct participants to take a pen or pencil from the table and to find a partner.

3. Tell them that one person in the pair will be the talker and one will be the listener. The talker must talk for one full minute (about anything he or she chooses); the listener holds up the listening stick (as a reminder of his or her role) and must only listen (no talking or adding anything verbal to the interaction, but nodding, smiling, and gestures are okay).

4. Ask pairs to choose roles and when everyone is ready, start the stopwatch and say, "Go."

5. After one minute, do a quick debriefing with the discussion questions below.

6. Have the pairs change roles, and tell the listening partner to raise his or her listening stick. Start the clock again for one more minute and say, "Go."

7. Debrief again, using the same questions below.

DISCUSSION QUESTIONS FOR DEBRIEFING

1. How did it feel to be the listener?

2. How did it feel to be the talker?

3. Did a minute feel like a long time?

4. Was anything about this exercise frustrating?

Learning Activity 10–5:
Active Listening Role Play

OBJECTIVE

The objective of this learning activity is to let participants experience and practice the skill of active listening.

Note: Conduct this activity after the content on active listening has been taught (chapter 7). It's most powerful if used in conjunction with Learning Activity 10–4: The Listening Stick because it provides experience at a deeper level of listening skill.

MATERIALS

◆ None

TIME

◆ 20 minutes

INSTRUCTIONS

1. Ask participants to choose a work-related challenge to talk about.

2. Have them form pairs and choose first-round roles—one talker, one listener.

3. Instruct the talkers to talk for five minutes about the challenge they've chosen. Instruct the listeners to use the skills of *active* listening throughout their partners' presentations.

4. When everyone is ready, begin the stopwatch and say, "Go."

5. After five minutes, call time and do a quick debriefing, using the questions below.

6. After debriefing, instruct the participants to change roles. Begin the stopwatch again.

7. Debrief again, using the same questions below.

VARIATION

You may choose to do this in triads, with one participant acting as an observer. If the participants form triads, ensure that the observer in the first round is a speaking or listening participant in the second round. It would be fine to have three rounds to accommodate all participants.

DISCUSSION QUESTIONS FOR DEBRIEFING

1. How did it feel to be the listener?

2. How did it feel to be the talker?

3. Did that feel like a long time?

4. How did it feel to use the active listening skills? Was it different than traditional listening?

5. Was anything frustrating about this exercise?

6. What did you discover as an observer of the exercise?

Learning Activity 10–6: Visual Listening

OBJECTIVE

The objective of this learning activity is to increase participants' awareness of the powers of observation and their importance in communication.

MATERIALS

♦ None

TIME

♦ 15 minutes

PREPARATION

Arrange the chairs back to back in pairs.

INSTRUCTIONS

1. Ask participants to select as a partner someone who has not been sitting beside them. (If participant numbers are uneven, you must partner with someone.)

2. Have the pairs sit back to back.

3. Give each participant in each pair 90 seconds to describe his or her partner's features and clothing to the partner. If you partner with someone, be sure to set your stopwatch at 90 seconds so you can advise the class when to switch the observations.

4. Allow two minutes for each pair to compare their discoveries with each other, to see whether they were correct or incorrect in their observations. Each person in the pair who described features correctly raises his or her hand and gets applause.

5. Debrief as a whole, using the discussion questions below.

VARIATION

Instead of asking partners to describe one another, ask them to recall and report one another's last question or comment made to the class.

DISCUSSION QUESTIONS FOR DEBRIEFING

1. How did you feel while you were being described [or while your question or comment was being repeated]?

2. How did you feel when you were describing your partner [or repeating his or her question or comment]?

3. What is important about observation in listening and communication?

Learning Activity 10–7: One on One

OBJECTIVE

The objective of this learning activity is to discuss a case study and evaluate the communication techniques used.

MATERIALS

◆ Tool 12–4: One on One

TIME

◆ 20 minutes

PREPARATION

Make a copy of Tool 12–4 for each participant.

INSTRUCTIONS

1. Pass out copies of Tool 12–4 and ask participants to form groups of four or five people.

2. Ask for a volunteer from each group to read the study aloud.

3. When the study has been read, instruct each group to discuss the study, using the questions below.

DISCUSSION QUESTIONS FOR DEBRIEFING

1. What are some potential areas of conflict?

2. What kind of listening has been used?

3. Have they used appropriate questioning skills?

4. What kinds of problems could be caused by the way Michael has handled communication in this situation?

5. Was the outcome successful?

6. How would you remake this scene?

Learning Activity 10–8:
Icebreaker: Class Reunion

OBJECTIVES

The objectives of this learning activity are to create high energy among the participants, enable them to greet each other with fun and enthusiasm, and let them experience both connected and disconnected communication.

MATERIALS

- None

TIME

- 10 minutes

INSTRUCTIONS

1. Ask participants to greet everyone in the room in a way that many of us have been greeted at networking events—with a cursory handshake, no personal connection, and no apparent interest.

2. Call time when they have completed this exercise.

3. Ask them now to imagine they all went to the same university and played in the same jazz ensemble. They know one another well and this is their five-year reunion. Ask them to greet each other accordingly.

4. Call time (when the shouting dies down) and discuss the exercise, using the following questions.

DISCUSSION QUESTIONS FOR DEBRIEFING

1. Which greeting did you prefer, the first or the second?

2. What are the differences between the two greetings?

3. How are the exercises similar to real-life communication?

Learning Activity 10–9: Interpersonal Skills

OBJECTIVE

The objective of this learning activity is to help participants understand and practice sensitive information exchange by depersonalizing it.

MATERIALS

   ◆   Paper and pen for all participants

TIME

   ◆   30 minutes

INSTRUCTIONS

1.   Give all participants five minutes to recall and write down brief details of a recent difficult workplace communication exchange in which the participant was on the receiving end of inflammatory statements.

2.   Have participants form groups of four.

3.   Have each participant, in turn, describe his or her situation to the group, carefully omitting the pronouns *I, me,* and *my* in the telling. Instruct the listening members of each group to keep the speaker on track by identifying use of any of the pronouns. They can do this by lightly tapping the table or raising a hand when a pronoun is used.

4.   Ask a spokesperson from each group to explain to the whole class the group's reactions and responses to the objectivity required and displayed by the omission of pronouns.

5.   Discuss the exercise, using the following questions.

DISCUSSION QUESTIONS FOR DEBRIEFING

1.   Is it challenging to speak of personal experiences from an objective viewpoint?

2.   What are the benefits of speaking objectively?

3.   In what situations could you use this skill in your workplace?

Learning Activity 10–10: I Want It!

OBJECTIVE

The objective of this learning activity is to let participants experience the frustration that occurs in persuasion and negotiation exchanges when one's needs are not being met.

MATERIALS

* None

TIME

* 5 minutes

INSTRUCTIONS

Note: You may wish to role-play this activity with a volunteer from the class before inviting all participants to get involved.

1. Ask participants to select a partner and stand face to face.

2. Number each partner 1 or 2.

3. Tell partner 1 to silently choose something he or she has or owns that will not be given away, no matter how much someone else negotiates for it. This might be a painting, a child, a car, or a job, for example. Tell partner 1 that the only phrase he or she can use is "You can't have it."

4. Tell partner 2 that he or she desperately wants whatever partner 1's item is (although the item is not revealed or described). Instruct them to use only the phrase "I want it."

5. Advise participants that they can become loud, emotional, conniving, and theatrical in their demands.

6. Call time after 90 seconds and ask partners to swap roles. Remind them of the only phrases they may use.

7. Call time after 90 seconds and ask partners to shake hands.

8. Reform as a whole group and discuss the activity, using the following questions.

DISCUSSION QUESTIONS FOR DEBRIEFING

1. How did you feel as the "owner"?

2. How did you feel as the "demander"?

3. How closely did this exercise emulate real-life communication challenges?

Learning Activity 10–11: Ten Questions About Conflict

OBJECTIVE

The objective of this learning activity is to have the participants give thought to a conflict situation and prepare some target questions. This activity will help reveal a person's major concerns about a situation.

MATERIALS

- ◆ Paper and pen for each participant

TIME

- ◆ 30 minutes

INSTRUCTIONS

1. Ask each participant to take a few minutes to think about a conflict he or she is dealing with right now.

2. Have participants write 10 questions they would like to ask the person with whom they are in conflict.

3. If there is enough time, ask everyone to write 10 questions the other person would like to ask them.

4. Discuss the activity, using the following questions.

DISCUSSION QUESTIONS FOR DEBRIEFING

1. What did this activity reveal to you?

2. What is keeping you from asking these questions of the other person?

3. Is there a way you can appropriately ask these questions?

Learning Activity 10–12: Persuasion

OBJECTIVE

The objective of this learning activity is to give participants the opportunity to experience a situation in which persuasion is applied to achieve a specific result.

MATERIALS

♦ PowerPoint slide 8–18

TIME

♦ 30 minutes

INSTRUCTIONS

1. Begin by asking for a volunteer to leave the room. Be gentle and careful of feelings toward the person who leaves. Some participants are very comfortable leaving the rest of the class, but if a person volunteers because no one else in the class has done so, then explain that his or her departure from the room is vital to the successful outcome of the activity.

2. Show PowerPoint slide 8–18 and ask for a second volunteer, who will act as a "persuader."

3. Explain that the persuader's task is to persuade the volunteer outside to hand over an object of some value (for example, a watch, glasses, a pin, or necklace). The persuader will begin by making easy conversation with the person whose object he or she is trying to get by persuasion. Gradually the focus of the conversation will move to the desired object and the persuader's goal is to convince the owner to remove and hand over the object.

4. Change the slide and call the first volunteer back into the room. Ask the two participants to begin their role play.

5. Call time after five minutes and then discuss the experience as a class, using the questions below.

6. Note on the flipchart which skills cited in Tool 12–10 were effective in the persuasion.

DISCUSSION QUESTIONS FOR DEBRIEFING

1. How did the first volunteer feel throughout the activity?

2. How did the persuader feel throughout the activity?

3. If the activity was successful, at what point did the persuader begin to accomplish his or her persuasion task?

4. If the persuader was not successful, what went wrong?

Learning Activity 10-13: Persuasion Strategy

OBJECTIVES

The objectives of this learning activity are to identify a situation in which persuasion will be required and develop a strategic roadmap to handle that situation.

MATERIALS

◆ Paper and pen for each participant

TIME

◆ 30 minutes

INSTRUCTIONS

1. Ask participants to write brief details of a professional situation that will require persuasion skills (for example, adoption of a new HR policy, changes in a team, and so forth). This can be a real-life professional example or one that each participant makes up for the purpose of the activity.

2. Instruct participants to briefly describe characteristics of the person(s) who will need to be persuaded (for example, stubborn, fearful of change, dominant, sensitive, and the like).

3. When everyone has completed the first two steps, pair the participants.

4. Ask partners to assist each other in strategizing a plan that will produce optimum results in the situation.

5. Reassemble the class and ask people to share the plans they devised.

6. Debrief the exercise, using the following questions.

VARIATION

This activity could be given as a homework assignment, with the partnering taking place at the next workshop session.

DISCUSSION QUESTIONS FOR DEBRIEFING

1. Did you see your "big-picture" situation more clearly?

2. What are the benefits of writing out the situation before devising a plan to handle it?

3. Did you find yourself persuading your partner to accept your ideas for his or her situation?

4. Will you use this activity on your return to your workplace?

Learning Activity 10–14: Negotiation Outcomes

OBJECTIVE

The objective of this learning activity is to let the participants explore and discuss the elements of negotiation and complete a strategic plan to implement when they return to the workplace.

MATERIALS

- ◆ Paper and pen for each participant
- ◆ Flipchart and marking pen for each group of four people

TIME

- ◆ 35 minutes

INSTRUCTIONS

1. Ask participants to form groups of four people.

2. Give groups 10 minutes to discuss situations that will require negotiation (for example, lowering a vendor's price, moving a deadline, securing a promotion, and so forth).

3. Ask them to choose a situation and identify the desired or at least satisfactory result.

4. Instruct each group to determine the steps required to reach the result. Have someone from each group write the steps on the flipchart.

5. Select any one of the groups and have it present to the class the situation it tackled and the negotiation strategy it devised.

6. Discuss the activity, using the questions below.

DISCUSSION QUESTIONS FOR DEBRIEFING

1. Where do the roadblocks lie in negotiations?

2. What is required to keep a negotiation moving forward?

3. What are the "dos" and "don'ts" of negotiations?

4. What makes a good negotiator?

Learning Activity 10–15: Feedback Experience

OBJECTIVE

The objective of this learning activity is to enable participants to experience feedback directly and learn about themselves in the process.

MATERIALS

◆ Training Instrument 10–2: Feedback Questionnaire

TIME

◆ 45 minutes

PREPARATION

Make one copy of Training Instrument 10–2 for each participant.

INSTRUCTIONS

1. Distribute copies of Training Instrument 10–2.

2. Instruct participants to complete the questionnaire.

3. Ask the class to form groups of four people.

4. Explain that each person is to briefly share with the group his or her answers to questions 1 through 5. After each participant has contributed, one participant will ask another participant the following questions about item 3 on the feedback questionnaire:

   ◆ Why has feedback not been received already?

   ◆ What are you looking for as a result of the feedback?

   ◆ Have you identified a colleague who could give this feedback?

5. Tell the groups that while one person is questioning another, the remaining two people observe and after the questioning is concluded they comment to the questioner on his or her feedback skills. The questioner will advise when the "interview" is finished.

6. Reassemble the whole class to discuss the activity and to identify discoveries made and lessons learned.

Training Instrument 10–2
Feedback Questionnaire

Instructions: Answer the following questions as honestly as you can.

1. In the past, when I have received negative feedback I have felt

2. Feedback is something I *[circle one]* do / do not seek on a regular basis because

3. One area of my professional life that would benefit from feedback is

4. I *[circle one]* enjoy / do not enjoy giving negative feedback because

5. Lessons I have learned in this workshop that I will apply to giving and receiving feedback in the future include

DISCUSSION QUESTIONS FOR DEBRIEFING

1. Which was the more comfortable side of the feedback exchange—giving or receiving?

2. Did you leave your group with the sense that the person who was questioned would seek the feedback on return to the workplace?

3. Will you seek feedback?

4. What was the greatest insight you gained into the feedback process?

Learning Activity 10–16: Johari Window

OBJECTIVE

The objective of this learning activity is to extend participants' study of feedback so that they learn where their personal blind spots are.

MATERIALS

- ◆ Training Instrument 10–3: Johari Window

TIME

- ◆ 30–45 minutes

PREPARATION

Make a copy of Training Instrument 10–3 for each participant.

INSTRUCTIONS

Note: You may choose to role-play the exercise with a participant before the activity begins. It works well if you take the blind spot–receiving end of the interaction.

1. Pass out copies of Training Instrument 10–3 to participants.

2. Ask them to complete Boxes 1 and 3 with three simple phrases. For example, in Box 1: my name, my profession, my personality; in Box 3: something I would love to do or learn, what I'm currently reading, what I love to do when no one is watching me (these have to be facts that the participants don't mind sharing).

3. Have participants form pairs and discuss what they've written in Boxes 1 and 3.

4. Ask pairs to move to Box 2. Participants may seek information from their partners about one (or more) blind spots, depending on comfort levels. For example, one participant in the pair may want to tell his or her partner about the constant oral interruptions the partner makes in class or about laughing too loudly. This part of the activity takes a leap of faith and trust for and by each participant because he or she will be providing potentially sensitive information about the partner.

Training Instrument 10–3
Johari Window

Instructions: In Boxes 1 and 3, write simple phrases about yourself that fit the "knowing" criteria listed there. Seek information from a partner or colleague that you can place in Box 2.

1. I Know Others Know **Open/Public Self**	**2.** I Don't Know Others Know **Blind Spot**
3. I Know Others Don't Know **Private Self**	**4.** I Don't Know Others Don't Know **Unknown Self**

Source: Created by Joseph Luft and Harrington Ingham. Adapted from Joseph Luft, *Of Human Interaction.* Palo Alto, CA: National Press Books, 1969.

5. Direct each pair to form a group with another pair and discuss the exercise, using the following questions.

DISCUSSION QUESTIONS FOR DEBRIEFING

1. What was the best part of this activity?

2. Did you feel safe or threatened with your partner?

3. What will you do with the new information you have about yourself?

4. Could you do this exercise with others?

Learning Activity 10–17: Assertiveness—Making Your Case

OBJECTIVE

The objective of this learning activity is to help participants understand the meaning of assertiveness and its use in the workplace.

MATERIALS

- ◆ One case study

- ◆ Paper and pen for each participant

TIME

- ◆ 30 minutes

PREPARATION

Write one short case study (that is, less than 200 words) for the participants. The study should be an exchange between two people in a professional situation (for example, an employee seeking a raise or promotion, a supervisor giving performance feedback to a subordinate). Write the exchange in weak and nonassertive language. The point of writing the case study yourself is to make it more pertinent to the group. Only one case study is needed for this activity.

INSTRUCTIONS

1. Give all participants a copy of the case study and tell them that they will have 20 minutes to complete this activity.

2. Explain that the communication in the case study is in weak, non-assertive language, and that each class member is to rewrite the case study using assertive language.

3. When time has elapsed, ask volunteers to read their revised exchanges to the whole class.

4. As a whole group, discuss the activity, using the questions below.

VARIATION

Ask participants to break into groups of four people each and write a specific scenario in assertive language. Provide each group with a flipchart and marking pen to record their work. Then ask a member of each group to present its scenario to the class.

DISCUSSION QUESTIONS FOR DEBRIEFING

1. What is the most effective skill in assertiveness?

2. How can we convey the need for assertiveness in appropriate situations in the workplace?

3. How does assertiveness improve professional situations?

Learning Activity 10–18: Vocal Exercises

OBJECTIVE

The objective of this learning activity is to provide participants with voice and relaxation exercises that will enhance their communication skills delivery and results.

MATERIALS

- ◆ Tool 12–14: Fun Phrases and Tongue Twisters (optional)

TIME

- ◆ 30 minutes

INSTRUCTIONS

1. Ask participants to stand and give themselves plenty of room.

2. Ask each person to make a statement aloud in his or her normal voice. For example, "I am going to develop a strong, articulated voice."

3. Instruct everyone to take a deep nose breath, and then exhale it slowly. Repeat this three times. Do this with the class.

4. Instruct them to turn their necks from side to side to stretch the vocal cords and neck muscles and make them more flexible. Again, do this with the class to model the action.

5. Direct them to take a deep nose breath and, while holding it, raise their shoulders up beside their ears. Tell them to drop their shoulders as they exhale. Repeat three times. Model the actions as they do them.

6. Have them shake first their hands and then their feet vigorously to loosen up the body. Do this with them.

7. Tell everyone to take a deep nose breath and then exhale while saying "Hmmm-aaah." Do this with the class. Explain that this brings the voice forward and provides clarity of tone.

8. Instruct participants to vibrate their lips together (think of "horse lips") to provide flexibility for articulation. Repeat several times. Model the action and accompany the class.

9. Tell participants to stretch their mouths into a wide "AH" shape, followed by a strong "OO" shape. Repeat this action several times with the class. Explain that these movements provide jaw flexibility.

10. Instruct everyone to take another deep nose breath and exhale from the diaphragm on several "HA's." Do this with the group. Explain that this breathing produces a strong, vibrant voice.

11. Ask each participant to make the following statement to the class: "I now have a good, strong, well-articulated voice." Ask the participants to listen for changes in vocal tone and openness.

12. Discuss the activity, using the questions below.

VARIATION

For further practice, add to the exercises the tricky phrases and tongue-twisters in Tool 12–14.

 ## DISCUSSION QUESTIONS FOR DEBRIEFING

1. How did you feel after the exercises?

2. Did your voice feel stronger and more confident after the exercises?

3. What results do you expect in yourself during meetings and presentations when you practice these exercises beforehand?

Learning Activity 10–19: Storytelling

OBJECTIVES

The objectives of this learning activity are to promote the skills of storytelling as a valuable exercise in professional situations and to offer participants the chance to practice storytelling in the workshop.

MATERIALS

- ◆ Paper and pen

TIME

- ◆ 30 minutes

PREPARATION

Create or select a story that you can tell to the class to begin the exercise and illustrate the steps of the activity. For example, you might tell of an experience you had in front of an audience—perhaps when your mind went blank or you tripped on a microphone cord and almost fell on the stage (as Jenni did). Tell how you recovered in plain sight. Or tell a story of one of your earliest (and perhaps embarrassing) experiences in front of a class. The goal here is to have the story be memorable for the participants so that they are persuaded to draw memorable stories from their own experiences.

INSTRUCTIONS

1. Tell your story as a way of modeling the activity for the class.

2. Ask participants to identify an experience or incident from their work life or leisure time that makes a good story.

3. Give them five minutes to draft an outline and the details of the story. The following sample outline will help with this activity:

   - ◆ Identify the incident (tripping on microphone cord).

   - ◆ Describe the environment (an audience of 500 people in a convention center meeting room).

   - ◆ Identify the audience and/or personal reaction (they gasped and so did I).

- Explain how you saved the situation (I asked if anyone knew of a good speech coach because I needed one).

- Define the lesson learned from the incident (I am very careful with microphone cords now).

4. Divide participants into groups of four people.

5. Explain that each group member will have three minutes to tell his or her story to the others in the group. After each story, the three listeners will tell the details back to the storyteller to indicate whether the concepts were understood.

6. When everyone has had a chance to tell a story to the group, re-assemble the class as a whole and discuss the activity, using the following questions.

 ### DISCUSSION QUESTIONS FOR DEBRIEFING

1. What are the elements of a good story?

2. What does a story provide that facts alone do not? And why is that true?

3. What develops between the teller and the audience following a story?

Learning Activity 10–20: Analogies

OBJECTIVE

The objective of this learning activity is to teach people to disseminate complex information in a simple manner so as to accelerate listeners' understanding.

MATERIALS

- ◆ Flipchart and marking pen for each group

- ◆ Prize for each member of the winning group (optional)

TIME

- ◆ 20 minutes

PREPARATION

Prepare a list of analogy examples (for example, teamwork is analogous to a baseball game; freeways are like the bloodstream).

INSTRUCTIONS

1. Define "analogy" and present some examples to ensure that the term and principles are understood.

2. Divide the class into two groups. Give each group a flipchart and a marking pen.

3. Ask each group to select a "scribe" who will record the group's work on the flipchart.

4. Give them 10 minutes to develop as many analogies as they can.

5. Read aloud the analogies on each groups' flipchart and award prizes to the group with the most analogies.

6. Give everyone a few minutes to write down the analogies from both groups.

7. Reassemble the groups as a whole and discuss the activity, using the following questions.

DISCUSSION QUESTIONS FOR DEBRIEFING

1. What makes analogies easier to understand than the facts?

2. Did this exercise get easier the more you did it? If so, why? If not, why not?

3. Did you see pictures forming during the telling of the analogy?

Assessments

What's in This Chapter?

- Client Survey and Needs Analysis
- Participant Survey and Needs Analysis
- Supervisor's Evaluation of Employee Participant
- Listening Skills Assessment
- Interpersonal Skills Assessment
- Negotiation Skills and Readiness Assessment
- Course and Facilitator Evaluation
- Learning Comprehension Level Assessment
- Skills Mastery Assessment
- Skills Application Assessment

Assessments and evaluations are vital to the life of a workshop, both before it begins and after it concludes. To design a workshop that is appropriate for your participants, you have to assess their needs and those of their organization. The needs analysis assessments in this chapter help you define the focus, goals, and desired outcome for your workshop.

By assessing the needs of your client company or the organization that hired you to facilitate the workshop, you have a better opportunity to meet those specific requirements. Frequently you will see differences in expectations between the organization and its participants. Therefore, discovering such discrepancies before your course begins ensures that you can take the appropriate steps to align the expectations.

Using assessments during the workshop helps participants identify their areas of strength and weakness, which leads to their discovery of the skills they should acquire or improve for the workplace.

An assessment of the workshop and the facilitator is vital both for the hiring organization and for you as the facilitator. To learn if you met the goals and expectations, you want direct responses from the participants. Negative comments in evaluations, even though they can be tough to read, ultimately ensure that you will improve or change some of your facilitation approaches in your next workshop.

Assessment 11–1
Client Survey and Needs Analysis

Instructions: Send this assessment by email or regular mail to the client company or organization at least one month before you begin the course. The answers supplied will give you a big-picture orientation to the needs of the company and the learning fundamentals required for the participants.

1. How many participants will attend?_____

2. What are their names and roles within the company/organization? *[Please attach an additional sheet if necessary.]*

_____

_____

_____

_____

_____

3. What is (are) the desired result(s) from the workshop?

_____

_____

_____

4. Will any participants have separate/different goals from that/those enumerated in question 3 above? If so, what are those goals?

_____

_____

_____

5. Will the workshop environment be formal or informal?_____

6. Will any participants be uncomfortable with this workshop? If yes, please state the reasons.

_____

_____

_____

continued on next page

Assessment 11–1, continued
Client Survey and Needs Analysis

7. Has your company/department participated in a similar workshop in the past? If so, please provide details of that workshop.

_____

_____

_____

8. Will all participants be able to dedicate the full time required to attend the workshop or will some leave before completion?

_____

9. How do participants work most effectively?

   ☐ Individually

   ☐ In pairs

   ☐ In small groups

   ☐ In a mix of the above

10. What follow-up action will you require from the facilitator?

_____

_____

_____

11. Additional information that will assist the facilitator:

_____

_____

_____

_____

_____

_____

_____

continued on next page

Assessment 11–1, continued
Client Survey and Needs Analysis

Training room set-up

☐ U-Shape (preferred)

☐ Team-style (2nd choice)

If you require the participants from your organization to be videotaped during the public speaking module of this course, please provide the following information:

1. Do you have the necessary audiovisual equipment available for the workshop?

   ☐ Yes

   ☐ No

2. Checkmark the following items if they are available at your location:

   ☐ Video camera

   ☐ Tripod

   ☐ Playback equipment

   ☐ Television monitor (for viewing videotapes)

   ☐ VHS videotapes (one per participant)

3. Handout materials will be provided by_____

Please email or fax this survey to [Facilitator name and contact information].

Assessment 11–2
Participant Survey and Needs Analysis

Instructions: It is important to understand the needs of the participants who will attend your workshop. Although you may not be able to fulfill all their needs in the course, this assessment will make you aware of their interests and requirements and you will be able to keep these in mind while working with them.

1. The communication topics I would like to explore in a communication skills workshop are *[check all that apply]:*

    ☐ Listening

    ☐ Conflict resolution

    ☐ Assertiveness

    ☐ Internal vs. external communication

    ☐ Upward vs. downward communication

    ☐ Interpersonal communication

    ☐ Other_____

2. If I had to write the three most important topics in order of importance, the order would be

    a. _____

    b. _____

    c. _____

3. Is this selection defined by me or by my supervisor?

    _____

4. Is the culture of the company or organization one of open or closed communication?

    _____

Please write additional comments:

_____

_____

_____

continued on next page

Assessment 11–2, continued
Participant Survey and Needs Analysis

5. In a workshop I like to receive information in the following ways *[check all that apply]:*

   ☐ Lecture from facilitator   ☐ Discussion in pairs

   ☐ Study from workshop manual   ☐ Learning activities

   ☐ Whole-group discussion   ☐ PowerPoint presentation

   ☐ Small-group discussion   ☐ A blend of all the above

   ☐ Other_____

6. Have you attended a communications workshop in the past?_____
   If so, what topics were covered?

   _____

   _____

   What were the positive and negative aspects of the workshop?

   _____

   _____

7. What results will my organization or my supervisor expect to see in me following a
   communications workshop?

   _____

   _____

8. What personal results do I expect?

   _____

   _____

9. Additional information that will assist the workshop facilitator:

   _____

   _____

   _____

Thank you for the input! Your information will be treated confidentially.

Assessment 11–3
Supervisor's Evaluation of Employee Participant

Instructions: This assessment is focused on the requirements of the participants' supervisors. It is especially useful for discovering discrepancies between the supervisor's evaluation of the participant's needs and the participant's own perceived needs. If you discover during the course of the workshop that there are glaring discrepancies between the supervisor and participant needs, personally contact the supervisor following the completion of the workshop to discuss the inconsistency.

1. In what professional situations is the employee required to exhibit clear and concise communication?

2. In what areas does the employee experience the greatest challenges in communication?

3. What are the employee's communication strengths?

4. Which skills would you recommend that this employee learn in a communications workshop?

5. What results do you expect for this employee following the communications workshop?

6. How will you support the continued development of the employee after the conclusion of the workshop?

Additional information that will assist the facilitator of the workshop:

Assessment 11–4
Listening Skills

Instructions: Mark the response that most closely matches your *typical* behavior. Be honest!

	USUALLY	OCCASIONALLY	SELDOM
1. When speaking with an associate, I finish his/her sentences.	☐	☐	☐
2. I interrupt an associate who explains something to me before he/she has finished speaking.	☐	☐	☐
3. I ask questions to be sure that I understand.	☐	☐	☐
4. I am quick to defend myself if an associate complains to me about something I have done or not done.	☐	☐	☐
5. I look beyond the words the speaker is using to mannerisms and tone.	☐	☐	☐
6. If I'm not interested in my conversation partner's topic, it shows in my facial/body expressions.	☐	☐	☐
7. I can remain neutral and not be prejudiced in my reactions to a speaker.	☐	☐	☐
8. I get distracted easily when I should be listening.	☐	☐	☐
9. I can remain calm even if the speaker is angry.	☐	☐	☐
10. I anticipate what the speaker will say and I stop listening.	☐	☐	☐
11. I make quick judgments while listening.	☐	☐	☐
12. I leave a discussion and find I cannot remember what my discussion partner said.	☐	☐	☐

How I feel when I have not been listened to:

_____

_____

What I can change about my listening approach:

_____

_____

_____

Assessment 11–5
Interpersonal Skills

Instructions: One of the most effective means for you to assess improvement in your communication skills is to complete the following assessment after you have collaborated in a meeting.

1. How have my reactions and responses changed following the meeting?

2. How will this meeting help me achieve greater professional effectiveness?

3. Do I now have a stronger relationship with that person/those people in the meeting?

4. Do I trust them? Do they trust me?

5. Through collaboration, could we achieve success on both sides of our partnership?

6. What leadership lesson have I learned from this interpersonal exchange?

Assessment 11–6
Negotiation Skills and Readiness

Instructions: Complete this assessment after you complete the negotiation exercise. It will give you the immediate opportunity to assess your negotiation style and preferences and will provide you with knowledge of the areas you might choose to improve.

1. What is (are) my greatest strength(s) in negotiation?

2. What are my weaknesses?

3. What will I remember to do differently next time?

4. What information will I benefit from having before I enter into negotiation?

5. What did I learn about myself when under pressure?

6. What personal skills will I employ to enhance my future negotiations?

7. What details of a negotiation will I undertake following the conclusion of this workshop?

Assessment 11–7

Course and Facilitator Evaluation

Name (optional):_____ **Date**_____

Instructions: Answer the following questions to provide important feedback to the facilitator about his or her facilitation work and about the content of the workshop. You do not have to include your name if you prefer not to do so. Please leave the evaluation in the room when you go.

1. Did the workshop meet your expectations? If not, why not?

2. Was *[name]* an effective facilitator? If not, why not?

3. Were the materials appropriate and applicable?   ☐ Yes ☐ No

4. Did the facilitator have a good understanding of the material?   ☐ Yes ☐ No

5. Did the facilitator respond to questions and lead an interactive workshop?   ☐ Yes ☐ No

6. What three skills will you take from this workshop?

7. Were there any elements you did not like?

8. How would you change this workshop?

9. Was this training worthwhile?   ☐ Yes ☐ No

10. Would you invite this facilitator back to lead another workshop?   ☐ Yes ☐ No

11. Additional comments:

Assessment 11–8
Learning Comprehension Level

Instructions: Answer the following questions as fully as possible. This assessment will help you identify your level of comprehension of the materials covered in this workshop.

1. Give a brief overview of your learning in this workshop. Begin your statements with "I have learned...." This will help you focus your responses.

2. How and where will you apply this knowledge in your workplace?

3. Did you acquire this knowledge through lectures, practice, discussion, or a combination of all methods?

4. Do you feel sufficiently confident to pass on this knowledge to your colleagues?

5. Are there any knowledge areas that will require additional learning in order for you to feel confident?

Assessment 11–9
Skills Mastery

Instructions: Answer the following questions as fully as you can. The questions are designed to assess your mastery of communication skills.

1. If you were asked to teach one skill in this workshop, which skill would you choose?

2. What would your three key message points be in teaching the skill?

3. Describe the steps you would take to teach each message point (for example, lecture, group discussion, PowerPoint presentation, and so forth).

4. What methods would you use to ensure that your colleagues understood your instruction?

5. Would both positive and negative feedback from your colleagues affect the development of your skills mastery? If yes, explain how and why that would happen and describe what changes you would make.

Assessment 11–10
Skills Application

Instructions: Answer the following questions as fully as you can. The questions will help you identify the extent of your ability to apply the skills you've learned in the workshop.

1. Describe a situation at your workplace in which you could employ one specific communication skill from this workshop.

2. How will you introduce this skill to your colleagues?

3. How will you set goals to measure the improvement from this skill?

4. Describe the input and participation you will expect from your colleagues.

5. How will you exemplify mastery of the skill?

Tools

- ◆ Twenty tools to enhance communication skills workshops and to support the learning when participants are back on the job

The following tools offer practical communication reminders and strategies that can be used regularly in the workplace. Encourage participants to share these with their colleagues or co-workers. Doing so furthers the opportunity to improve communication in the workplace.

By practicing the exercises contained in the tools, participants gain a more comprehensive grasp of them, and accordingly are better able to put them to use. It is commonly held that practicing a skill five times a day for 21 days will make it a habit. When participants leave a workshop with these tools for their use in the workplace, there is a greater chance that the skills will become habits for them, thereby enhancing their overall communication.

Tool 12–1
Frequently Used Action Verbs

You may wish to write these verbs on a flipchart page and hang it on the classroom wall. The list is a resource for participants during the workshop. These verbs are also used in chapter 9 as part of the vocal exercises activity.

Analyze	Determine	Initiate	Report
Appraise	Develop	Inspect	Represent
Assemble	Direct	Instruct	Research
Assist	Discuss	Investigate	Review
Authorize	Distribute	Monitor	Schedule
Calculate	Draft	Notify	Select
Collect	Establish	Obtain	Specify
Compile	Estimate	Participate	Submit
Conduct	Evaluate	Perform	Supervise
Consult	Execute	Plan	Train
Coordinate	Exercise	Practice	Verify
Correspond	Formulate	Prepare	
Delegate	Implement	Provide	
Design	Improve	Recommend	

Tool 12–2

Journal Pages

My goals for this workshop:

1. _____

2. _____

3. _____

4. _____

5. _____

---

1. Which skills have I learned that will be the most useful for me?

2. Where will I apply these skills?

3. How will I keep practicing these skills?

continued on next page

Tool 12–2, continued
Journal Pages

4. How will I pass these skills on to others in my workplace?

5. Do I have/will I find a mentor who will help me focus these skills and keep me accountable? *[Identify a person/role and reasons for mentoring selection.]*

Additional thoughts

Goals for specific development

Tool 12-3
Tips for Understanding Body Language

Our body language speaks constantly. According to Dr. Albert Mehrabian, the author of *Silent Messages,* 50 percent of our communication cues are visual.

Here are some frequently used body signals:

BODY LANGUAGE	THE MESSAGE
Standing or sitting with tightly folded arms and crossed feet	Feeling skeptical or defensive*
Chin stroking	Making a decision
Cheek resting on fist, index finger pointing upward	Listening with interest
Hands clasped at chin, elbows on table	Feeling defensive or making an evaluation
Rubbing hands together	Feeling excitement or optimism
Holding hand over mouth	Skepticism, evaluation, or suppressing deceit
Chewing tips of fingers	Feeling anxiety

*This body language is also used when a person is feeling physically cold, so use caution with your interpretation.

Tool 12–4

One on One

The following scenario describes an employee's termination from his job after absences from work. The communication between the supervisor and the employee misses several steps that would ensure a more effective handling of sensitive news. Please explore this scenario, define the missing communication steps, and develop the scenario into an effective exchange that ensures that the employee understands why he is being terminated.

SCENARIO

Michael is the supervisor in the accounting department, and Robert works as an accounting assistant. The company's attendance policy permits three absences in one calendar year. Robert has been absent or tardy many times and he is nearing possible termination. To this point, Michael has given only verbal warnings when Robert was absent or late, but Robert's behavior is repeating itself so Michael sets up a meeting with Robert to discuss the situation. Here is the exchange:

Robert: "Sorry I was late. I won't let it happen again."

Michael: "That's all well and good, but it is setting a bad example for the rest of the department."

Robert: [Thinking: *Great, he's not really very mad. I'm probably not in very much trouble after all. He's just blowing off steam.*]

Michael: "If this happens again, I'll be forced to let you go. Does that sound unfair?"

Robert: "No, I don't have any problem with that." [Thinking: *This guy's a push-over. He'd never do that.*]

Michael: "Well, I'm glad we had this discussion and that we both understand the consequences."

Two weeks later Robert misses a day of work. Witness the meeting he has with Michael when he returns to his job the following day:

Michael: "Robert, here's your final check. Please clear out your desk and security will escort you out."

Robert: "Why are you firing me? I just missed a day of work!"

Tool 12–5

Maslow's Hierarchy of Needs

Abraham Maslow designed the Hierarchy of Needs in the early 1950s to describe a theory of motivation based on fulfilling successively higher levels of human needs. The most elemental of our needs are physiological: food, drink, shelter, and sexual satisfaction. The second step up the hierarchy is the need for safety, for shelter and protection from physical and emotional harm so that we may develop emotionally and physiologically. The third level of needs are social ones—for love and a sense of belonging from our parents, siblings, or extended families in order to realize our individual self. The next level of need is for esteem. Needs here are both internal (for example, self-respect and autonomy) and external (for example, status and attention). When we are comfortable with ourselves we seek recognition from others that helps us define our place in society and in the global community. Finally we work to gain self-actualization, which is a "knowing" about life and its meaning for us and a sense that we fit into the paradigm. We seek to realize our full potential through satisfying relationships and professional roles, and much of this we achieve through effective communication.

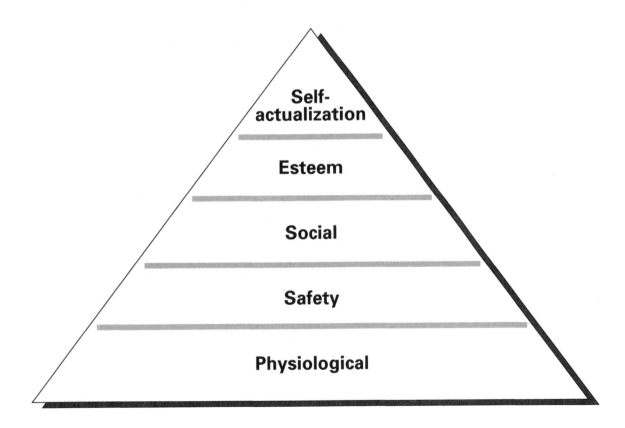

Source: Abraham H. Maslow, *Motivation and Personality,* 2nd ed. New York: Harper and Row, 1970.

Tool 12–6

Nonconfrontational Language—Using "I" Rather Than "You"

When people are emotional about a situation, they often become aggressive and abrupt, using language that attacks another person rather than language that takes responsibility for their role or at least their feelings. "I" messages are a way to communicate thoughts and feelings in a non-aggressive manner.

Here are some examples of how you can convert a confrontational "You" message into a more effective "I" message.

"YOU" MESSAGE	"I" MESSAGE
You really wrecked the project when you took over.	I feel very upset about the direction the project has taken since you took over.
I can't believe you did that!	I am really upset about the decision you made.
You don't even care about the success of this project.	I feel disappointed because it seems like you are not concerned about the success of the project.

Tool 12–7
Skills for Interpersonal Success

What follows are guidelines for developing successful interpersonal skills:

* Work on your own self-awareness. Stop making others villains and yourself a victim.

* Stop trying to win arguments and start trying to find common ground. Seek win–win solutions.

* Listen well. Invite the ideas of others.

* Carefully share your feelings and opinions. Invite others to do the same.

* Express your ideas as opinions rather than as "the truth." That makes what you say easier for others to digest.

* Be exceedingly honest with yourself, and with others.

* Set specific goals for improving your interpersonal skills.

Tool 12–8

Pointers for Developing Interpersonal Skills and the Benefits of Doing So

In a communication exchange, when one person is trying to draw information from another or help someone see the big picture, open-ended questions require "accountability" in the answer. In other words, because the identifying question doesn't judge or stipulate an outcome, the receiver is able to provide input and information from his or her perspective.

1. Identify the challenge by asking open-ended questions that begin with

   ◆ "What can we . . . ?"

   ◆ "How would you . . . ?"

   ◆ "Does the situation . . . ?"

   ◆ "Is there a better way to . . . ?"

2. Starting questions with "Why?" raises defenses and creates an impasse.

3. Asking open-ended questions motivates buy-in from the other person.

4. The goal of successful interpersonal strategies is to reach a win–win resolution. That doesn't mean that the other person will get his or her way, but finding a way in which both parties can embrace the outcome makes a difference in the reaction to discipline and change.

5. Be accountable for your actions.

6. Lead by example.

Benefits of Effective Interpersonal Strategies

◆ Reactions change

◆ Productivity increases

◆ Stronger relationships form

◆ Successful communication is experienced by both parties

◆ Trust increases

◆ Leadership capability is recognized

Tool 12-9

Five Steps to Resolving Conflict

Some people enjoy conflict. They react to it as a means of having their say or of putting their viewpoint across with strength and conviction. For those people who do not enjoy conflict, either one-on-one or in group situations, the following steps provide guidance for finding a win–win resolution. The use of open-ended questions (discussed in Tool 12–8) will help identify the conflict issue.

Step 1. Define the problem.

Step 2. Clarify expectations and identify key players.

Step 3. Identify action steps to be taken.

Step 4. Resolve to take the agreed action steps.

Step 5. Follow up to ensure the action steps have solved the problem.

Tool 12–10

Persuasion Guidelines

Persuasion is a widely used technique in the professional world. When any one of us believes we have a good idea, we set about persuading others to buy into it also. However, if our "opposition" is not convinced that our idea is worthwhile, then persuasion becomes an important tool. Always remember in persuasion that you may not win, and that you must be ever mindful of the other person's point of view. Therefore, the following techniques should be employed for a successful exchange:

- Active listening skills are required of the persuader because he or she must be aware of the objections coming from the other person.

- Empathy should be conveyed by the persuader for the other person's point of view.

- Persuasion requires an ability to communicate effectively. The persuader must include appropriate benefits for the receiver, which means understanding the other person's needs and requirements.

- People usually need time to think when new ideas are being introduced. A decision in favor of the persuader may never be made, or it might not be made on the spot. The persuader must always have a timeframe in which he or she expects a result or an answer.

- Patience goes hand in hand with time. If the persuader tries to push the idea along faster than the receiver can process it to his or her satisfaction, an impasse may result.

- Use appropriate vocal and body tones. When the receiver is overwhelmed by urgent or pushy oral and body language, he or she could set up a barrier that prevents the flow of communication. Open, approachable body language with oral language to match will allow the idea to penetrate more effectively.

- Adopt a willingness to deal with conflict. Even when persuasive communication is being handled appropriately and effectively, it can escalate into conflict. (Tool 12–9 details techniques for dealing with conflict when it arises.)

Tool 12–11
Negotiation Strategies

◆ Be sure you understand the issues and facts of the negotiation topic. Successful negotiation requires a strong foundation. Identify your desired outcome and know where you will be willing to compromise.

◆ Know your negotiation partners. Consider their communication styles. How do they like to communicate? Do they prefer conflict? Will they be willing to compromise? What's in it for them?

◆ Negotiate only the issue at hand. Do not drag up old issues or past occurrences because this will weaken and possibly jeopardize your current topic.

◆ Be aware of your own oral and body language and those of your negotiation partners. Use open, positive hand gestures; maintain eye contact; and speak clearly and slowly. Be mindful of the language of your negotiation partners, and if you sense discomfort, ask open-ended questions related to the topic.

◆ If at any time in the negotiation you sense that you are gaining an edge, do not use this situation against your partners. Stay calm and focused on the outcome.

◆ When an outcome is reached by both/all parties, review the steps to be taken next. If an opposing party asks questions or wishes to negotiate further, be sure to answer all questions fully. If a decision is reached in your favor, show respect through appreciation and acknowledgment of others' participation in the discussion.

◆ Be sure that everyone understands the outcome and the follow-up steps. This is vital to a successful negotiation. Summarize in writing and get signatures of both parties where necessary. Follow up with phone calls or emails to ensure that the appropriate steps and procedures agreed to in the negotiation are being followed.

Tool 12–12
Simple Guidelines for Giving Feedback

In the professional world, feedback can be a very powerful tool for growth and development. However, it can also be perceived as negative and critical. Understanding how and when to give feedback applies a positive element to the exchange and establishes favorable working relationships. The following guidelines will assist you in this process:

1. Decide what specific feedback you want to give.

2. Respond quickly with feedback. Don't let the issue fester.

3. Keep your temper and your criticism in check.

4. Be respectful.

5. Focus on behavior that can be changed.

6. Use "I" statements.

7. Focus on helping the recipient succeed.

8. Follow up to ensure the feedback has been heard and understood.

9. Congratulate positive results.

Tool 12–13
Conflict in Team Meetings

The following budget-cutting scenario is unfortunately all too common in meeting rooms. If an atmosphere of suspicion and negativity is allowed to permeate the meeting, a successful result or decision cannot be reached. In this scenario, assertiveness is replaced by aggression, which leads to a lack of understanding and to subsequent conflict. Please review this scenario and reword it in a positive, assertive manner whereby a win–win situation can be reached.

MEETING SCENARIO

The staff at a major hospital is figuring out how to tighten the facility's belt after budget cuts. Ned has just made a suggestion that doesn't make a lot of sense, but at least he's trying to devise a way to deal with the problem.

Susan: "That's the stupidest thing I ever heard!"

Ned: "Well, Susan, I don't hear any brainstorms coming out of your mouth."

Sam, the supervisor: "Come on, you guys, let's try to keep this meeting on track. We're all in this together, and we need to make some changes to the work flow."

Susan: "Well, Ned is always kissing up, trying to look good. He's just hoping for the next promotion. He really doesn't care about this department."

Ned: "I'm the one who's always working after hours to get the job done. Don't tell me I don't care about this department, Susan. You go home the minute your shift is over."

Sam: "We're supposed to be coming up with an action plan to survive these budget cuts, and this arguing doesn't help at all. So stop it."

Susan: "I have no clue what to do about this. Our budget was cut 25 percent and there is no way we can do this job the same way anymore."

José: "Susan's right. We can't run this department on half the budget."

Ned: "How about if we—"

Susan: "Oh, great. Another one of Ned's ideas is coming!"

Sam: "Come on, Susan, you're not helping this situation at all. Let's try to get back on track and figure this out.

Tool 12-14
Fun Phrases and Tongue Twisters

It is very important in communication to have a clear, articulated voice. Incorrect interpretations can be made by receivers if they do not hear words or phrases correctly. This leads to confusion and misunderstanding. The following phrases not only require definite articulation (the use of lips, tongue, and jaw when pronouncing the words); they also provide a fun break for everyone in the workshop. Ensure that participants distinctly pronounce "t" and "d" sounds at the ends of words. When pronouncing an "L" the tongue should hit the ridge at the top of the mouth where the teeth meet the hard palate.

- Billy Button bought a buttered biscuit
- The painted pomp of pleasure's proud parade
- Like clocks, like locks
- Drowsy tinklings lull the distant folds
- Red leather, yellow leather
- A library literally littered with contemporary literature
- Katy caught a naughty kitten
- Helen heard the horses' hooves from her home on the hill
- Last night the cows prowled around the yard
- Dance past the last barn
- Park your car in Harvard Yard
- Proper copper coffee pot
- Mixed biscuits
- Six thistles
- Cup of cocoa
- Little kettles
- Purple metal
- Lovely yellow lilies
- Singing kettles
- Tipping teapots
- The Leith police dismisseth us

Tool 12–15
Delivery Skills for Effective Presentations

Successful presenting is not about me; it is about my audience.

A speaker who connects with his or her audience, engaging them in the topic and in the experience, demonstrates sophisticated communication skills. The ability to successfully convey information to an audience is a powerful skill. The following tools will help in the development of effective skills.

1. Breathe, relax, and loosen up before you speak. Remember that speaking is a performance. Prepare appropriately. Practice voice exercises (hmmaaah, "horse lips," and HA-HA-HA).

2. Adopt the "speaker-ready" stance. Place your weight on the balls of your feet. Imagine a string from the top of your head that reaches to the ceiling. Flex your knees. You are now centered for speaking.

3. Use the "steeple" for hand placement. The steeple places the tips of the fingers together in a "resting place." It conveys the coming together of ideas. It also gives the speaker confidence because of the element of touch. If the steeple feels too formal or stiff, interlock the fingers—a more relaxed gesture. Use the waist as the starting and resting place for your hands. Make positive, open-palmed gestures from waist-level and above. Extend your gestures beyond the parameters of your body. Use your hands to add energy and color. Avoid the "fig-leaf" stance (hands clasped with arms extended downward); don't rest your hands on your hips or put your hands in your pockets; and don't wring your hands.

4. Think of your speech as a conversation you're having with someone. The thought of speaking to an audience of more than 50 listeners can be very daunting for some people. Instead of thinking of them as an overwhelming number of 50, think of them as 1 person x 50. By doing this, you will speak to each person as though you are having a one-on-one conversation. This simplifies the process and enables the speaker to slowly gain confidence, one person at a time.

5. Make eye connection with your audience. Look at each person for three to five seconds and interact with him or her. Your message is written on the faces of your audience. When an audience member is absorbing your words and embracing your message, he or she will maintain eye contact with you. If there is agreement with what you are saying he or she may nod or smile or tip the head to one side. If the audience member disagrees, he or she will frown or turn away. As the speaker, if you are aware of the message behind these mannerisms you will continue when the responses are in agreement, and if you sense disagreement or doubt, you can stop and ask a question. For example, ask "Is there anything I can clarify at this point?" When you believe that your message is written on the faces of your audience you will stay focused on them and not start running an internal message that will take you away from the moment to the thoughts inside your head.

continued on next page

Tool 12–15, continued

Delivery Skills for Effective Presentations

6. Use the "Z" approach or divide the room into four segments when you speak to large audiences (more than 100 people). The Z approach to eye contact means starting at the back of the room first. (Always try to do this because the people in the back of a room are normally left out of contact by a speaker.) Slowly sweep your eyes along the back of the room to form the top of the Z. Then diagonally cross the room with your eye contact—the middle of the Z. Finally run your eyes across the front of the room, which forms the bottom of the Z. If you prefer to divide the room into four segments of a box, go to the back first and address a person in the "center" of the back left box. Then move laterally onto the next box and focus on the center person. Repeat this for the front two boxes also. In this context, the eye contact you maintain with the center person can increase to 10 seconds, which gives the people surrounding that person the feeling that you are speaking to them.

7. Remember that speaking is a 360° process. The effectiveness of your delivery is reflected by the audience. They, in turn, feed back their reactions to you.

8. Smile, use your eyes, and speak with your body. Bodies contain feelings, words contain thoughts. When you speak you deliver your thoughts. When you smile, use facial animation, or move, you are adding emotion to your message. A successful presentation needs both elements.

Tool 12–16
What Influences an Audience

When several of us walk into a meeting room carrying a message of importance to the company or organization, it is sad to say that the middle-aged, white male among us will carry the greatest influence. We cannot change (ostensibly) the first three bullet points below, but we can alter or enhance the remaining four bullet points through practice and development of self-esteem.

Here are the factors that influence an audience:

- Race
- Gender
- Age
- Posture, confidence, and space
- Eye contact, facial expression, and energy
- Appearance
- Handshake

Sometimes, who you are speaks so loudly,
I cannot hear what you are saying.
– Anonymous

Tool 12-17
Steps for Developing a Three-Point Presentation

There are many theories for the development of an effective presentation, but the one most frequently used and preferred is the method that uses three key message points. (This could also be referred to as a five-point presentation because the opening and conclusion are vital to the composition of the speech as well.) The following guidelines will help you develop a three-point presentation:

Step 1. Research and analyze your audience. Focus on what they want to/need to know and how they will benefit.

Step 2. Select your topic.

Step 3. Define your speech objective: to inform, advise, persuade, convince, instruct, show, promote, motivate.

Step 4. Write three key points that you will cover in your presentation.

Step 5. Add two to three subpoints for each main point.

Step 6. Wherever possible, use a story to illustrate one or more of the main points.

Step 7. Insert appropriate visual aids to enhance your message.

Step 8. Use your speech objective to create a dynamic opening. Options: Tell the audience something about yourself, ask rhetorical questions, use a powerful quotation, share a personal anecdote, or tell a story.

Step 9. Outline your key points at the beginning of the speech.

Step 10. Prepare a convincing conclusion that is tied to your objective. Summarize your key points.

Step 11. Transfer your key elements to note cards, held lengthwise. Write clearly. Highlight key points. Write reminders to breathe, smile, and connect.

Step 12. Practice your speech aloud, on your feet, in front of colleagues. Record yourself. Make smooth transitions from one point to the next. Ensure that your language is positive (for example, will, can, knows, does, is). If appropriate, use your company name whenever possible. Practice a conversational style.

Step 13. Remember that less is more! Eliminate unnecessary words and avoid repetition. Get to the point, and your audience will get your point.

Tool 12–18
All About Storytelling

Webster's Dictionary defines a story as a narration of an event; fictional prose intended to interest or amuse; an anecdote.

It defines an anecdote as a short and interesting or humorous account of a real or fictitious incident; previously unknown details of history or biography.

1. Use personal stories. If the incident happened to someone else, give credit.

2. Know *why* you are telling the story. Do not become a storyteller just to get the limelight. A story must have professional and timely relevance; in other words, it must further the learning experience for the audience.

3. Use the key line of the story to link back to your presentation. For example: "So this embarrassing experience of mine at the podium at the San Diego Convention Center, when I tripped on the microphone cord and ricocheted across the platform, should help you remember that when you are speaking, you are first and foremost a human being with foibles and frailties. Most audiences are forgiving. Allow them to forgive you by acknowledging you through laughter."

4. Use the moments after the audience has had a good laugh to get serious, speak to the minds and emotions of your listeners, ask for business (if getting business is your goal).

5. Practice your story. Do other people *really* laugh, get involved, and seem interested? If they do not, either rehearse the story endlessly with good friends or colleagues who will give you effective feedback, or drop the story.

6. Practice the "less is more" rule, and tell your story succinctly. Sometimes you need only a few sentences to recount the circumstances effectively.

7. Paint pictures with words. Speak to the senses. Here are some examples of sensory phrasing: the sound of water spilling over rocks, the sight of colorful birds soaring in flight, the taste of success.

8. Tell stories that fit *your* style. Emulation is flattering, but it doesn't always work if you decide to copy language that you do not use on a regular day, or if you deliver quotes from Shakespeare to embellish your story when you've never before spoken Shakespeare's lines.

Tool 12–19
Using Stories and Analogies

The use of stories and analogies in a presentation adds variety and interest. Even the most complex scientific or mathematical presentation is well served with stories and analogies. They break up routine, prevent monotony, engage the audience, and enable listeners to take away practical explanations for complicated topics. A personal story can inspire in a way that leads to some desired change for an audience member.

Stories are experiences. They highlight points you want to make. They bring color to a speech or presentation. They connect your subject and your audience.

Analogies are parallels. They are incidents or events that can be related to the point of your speech. They are useful for explaining complex ideas because they relate something unknown to something known.

There are stories and analogies everywhere. Start paying attention to them and practice weaving them into your presentations. Use descriptive language, energetic body language, and eye contact to tell them effectively.

If you're not certain if something is a story or an analogy, remember this example of a story: An experience you had on a job that tells how you mobilized a team or brought an idea to implementation.

And here's an example of an analogy: A baseball game is an analogy for teamwork.

Now try your hand at it:

◆ Driving to work on the freeway is an analogy for _____

It can be helpful to sit down and make a list of analogies and another list of personal stories that you might use in a presentation. Having this resource at your fingertips lets you build a dossier of your ideas and experiences, rather than having to seek them in books or on the Internet. You will be a sought-after speaker if you imbue your presentations with real-life examples and parallels that empower your audience.

Tool 12–20
Strategies for Effective Meetings

Meetings can strike fear in the hearts of professionals. "Oh, no, not another meeting!" is a common exclamation heard in corporations or organizations. Knowing how to run a successful meeting can make you sought after for your efficiency and courtesy.

You probably wouldn't invite people to your home for dinner without doing a few hours of preparation before your guests arrive. Therefore, preparation should be done before participants arrive at a meeting.

1. Appoint a facilitator and a timekeeper.

2. Create a "parking lot" for issues that can't be covered when they arise. Use the parking lot issues for the next meeting.

3. Call for a process check regularly. After two or three agenda items, depending on their length and complexity, ask the attendees these questions: "How are we doing? How is everyone feeling? Are we making progress?" This allows for reviews of the process at different intervals.

4. When an agenda item is completed, move on to the next and don't waste time. If all business is completed ahead of time, end the meeting. Don't feel that you have to drag it on until its usual completion hour, and don't linger after the meeting for an "after-meeting meeting."

5. Serve food.

6. Allow stretch time.

7. Let meeting participants drive the agenda. It helps the flow of a meeting to delegate specific agenda items to the participants, not only to the chair or other senior members. When people feel the meeting belongs to them, they will approach it and interact appropriately.

8. Meet outdoors or outside the work environment. When a meeting topic is challenging, working outside the usual meeting space can change the dynamics of interaction. Participants feel freer to speak and engage. Meeting away from the office prevents interruptions and distractions.

9. Model good meeting behavior. Courtesy should be practiced at meetings. This includes not speaking when others are speaking, listening actively, asking open-ended questions, drawing the more quiet participants into the conversation, and taking any urgent phone call outside the meeting room.

10. Give others' ideas precedence over yours.

11. Listen to everyone. Paraphrase, but don't judge their remarks.

12. Assume that everyone's ideas have value.

continued on next page

Tool 12–20, continued
Strategies for Effective Meetings

13. Control the dominant people without alienating them.

14. Let your interest and alertness be contagious.

15. Keep track of the agenda and advise the attendees of progress through it. Even with an agenda in front of them, participants in a meeting will lose track. From time to time, refer to the agenda item coming up for discussion, or recall a previous item to bring value to the current topic.

16. Check with anyone who "owns" a problem under discussion to find out if it is worth pursuing. Occasionally one topic will trigger another that is not on the agenda. If it carries importance for the participants, side conversations and discussions may arise. Check with the person responsible for the new topic to see if it needs to be discussed immediately. If not, table it for discussion later in the meeting or at the next meeting.

17. From time to time, ask other participants in the group to lead the meeting. This enables them to better understand the process and to provide feedback from their own experience. Remember this: Those who lead, learn.

Appendix

Using the Compact Disc

Insert the CD and locate the file *How to Use This CD.doc.*

Contents of the CD

The compact disc that accompanies this workbook on communication skills training contains three types of files. All of the files can be used on a variety of computer platforms.

- **Adobe .pdf documents.** These include assessments, figures, tables, tools, and training instruments.

- **Microsoft PowerPoint presentations.** These presentations add interest and depth to many of the training activities included in the workbook.

- **Microsoft PowerPoint files of overhead transparency masters.** These files makes it easy to print viewgraphs and handouts in black-and-white rather than using an office copier. They contain only text and line drawings; there are no images to print in grayscale.

Computer Requirements

To read or print the .pdf files on the CD, you must have Adobe Acrobat Reader software installed on your system. The program can be downloaded free of cost from the Adobe Website, *www.adobe.com.*

To use or adapt the contents of the PowerPoint presentation files on the CD, you must have Microsoft PowerPoint software installed on your system. If you simply want to view the PowerPoint documents, you must have an appropriate viewer installed on your system. Microsoft provides various viewers free for downloading from its Website, *www.microsoft.com.*

Printing From the CD

TEXT FILES

You can print the training materials using Adobe Acrobat Reader. Simply open the .pdf file and print as many copies as you need. The following .pdf documents can be directly printed from the CD:

- Assessment 11–1: Client Survey and Needs Analysis
- Assessment 11–2: Participant Survey and Needs Analysis
- Assessment 11–3: Supervisor's Evaluation of Employee Participant
- Assessment 11–4: Listening Skills
- Assessment 11–5: Interpersonal Skills
- Assessment 11–6: Negotiation Skills and Readiness
- Assessment 11–7: Course and Facilitator Evaluation
- Assessment 11–8: Learning Comprehension Level
- Assessment 11–9: Skills Mastery
- Assessment 11–10: Skills Application
- Tool 12–1: Frequently Used Action Verbs
- Tool 12–2: Journal Pages
- Tool 12–3: Tips for Understanding Body Language
- Tool 12–4: One on One
- Tool 12–5: Maslow's Hierarchy of Needs
- Tool 12–6: Nonconfrontational Language—Using "I" Rather Than "You"
- Tool 12–7: Skills for Interpersonal Success
- Tool 12–8: Pointers for Developing Interpersonal Skills and the Benefits of Doing So
- Tool 12–9: Five Steps to Resolving Conflict
- Tool 12–10: Persuasion Guidelines
- Tool 12–11: Negotiation Strategies
- Tool 12–12: Simple Guidelines for Giving Feedback
- Tool 12–13: Conflict in Team Meetings
- Tool 12–14: Fun Phrases and Tongue Twisters
- Tool 12–15: Delivery Skills for Effective Presentations
- Tool 12–16: What Influences an Audience
- Tool 12–17: Steps for Developing a Three-Point Presentation
- Tool 12–18: All About Storytelling

- ◆ Tool 12–19: Using Stories and Analogies
- ◆ Tool 12–20: Strategies for Effective Meetings
- ◆ Training Instrument 5–1: Personal Action Plan for Improving Your Communication Skills
- ◆ Training Instrument 9–1: Evaluation of a Presentation
- ◆ Training Instrument 10–1: The Circle of Influence
- ◆ Training Instrument 10–2: Feedback Questionnaire
- ◆ Training Instrument 10–3: Johari Window

POWERPOINT SLIDES

You can print the presentation slides directly from this CD using Microsoft PowerPoint. Simply open the .ppt files and print as many copies as you need. You can also make handouts of the presentations by printing three "slides" per page. These slides will be in color, with design elements embedded. Power-Point also permits you to print these in grayscale or black-and-white, although printing from the overhead masters file will yield better black-and-white representations. Many trainers who use personal computers to project their presentations bring along viewgraphs just in case there are glitches in the system. The overhead masters can be printed from the PowerPoint .pps files.

Adapting the PowerPoint Slides

You can modify or otherwise customize the slides by opening and editing them in the appropriate application. However, you must retain the denotation of the original source of the material—it is illegal to pass it off as your own work. You may indicate that a document was adapted from this workbook, written by Maureen Orey and Jenni Prisk and copyrighted by ASTD. The files will open as "Read Only," so before you adapt them you will need to save them onto your hard drive under a different file name.

Showing the PowerPoint Presentations

On the CD, the following PowerPoint presentations are included:

- ◆ One-Hour.ppt
- ◆ Half-Day.ppt
- ◆ Full-Day.ppt
- ◆ Two-Day.ppt.

Table A–1

Navigating Through a PowerPoint Presentation

KEY	POWERPOINT "SHOW" ACTION
Space bar *or* Enter *or* Mouse click	Advance through custom animations embedded in the presentation
Backspace	Back up to the last projected element of the presentation
Escape	Abort the presentation
B *or* b	Blank the screen to black
B *or* b *(repeat)*	Resume the presentation
W *or* w	Blank the screen to white
W *or* w *(repeat)*	Resume the presentation

Having the presentations in .ppt format means that they automatically show full-screen when you double-click on a file name. You also can open Microsoft PowerPoint and launch the presentations from there.

Use the space bar, the enter key, or mouse clicks to advance through a show. Press the backspace key to back up. Use the escape key to abort a presentation. If you want to blank the screen to black while the group discusses a point, press the B key. Pressing it again restores the show. If you want to blank the screen to a white background, do the same with the W key. Table A–1 summarizes these instructions.

We strongly recommend that trainers practice making presentations with the PowerPoint slides before using them in live training situations. You should be confident that you can cogently expand on the points featured in the presentations and discuss the methods for working through them. If you want to engage your training participants fully (rather than worrying about how to show the next slide), become familiar with this simple technology *before* you need to use it. A good practice is to insert notes into the *Speaker's Notes* feature of the PowerPoint program, print them out, and have them in front of you when you present the slides.

For Further Reading

Booher, Dianna. *Communicate with Confidence, How to Say It Right the First Time and Every Time*. New York: McGraw-Hill, 1994.

Burn, Bonnie E. *Flip Chart Power, Secrets of the Masters*. San Diego, CA: Jossey-Bass/Pfeiffer, 1996.

Burn, Bonnie, and Maggi Payment. *Assessments A to Z*. San Diego, CA: Jossey-Bass/Pfeiffer, 2000.

Covey, Stephen. *Seven Habits of Highly Effective People*. New York: Simon and Schuster, 1989.

Dowling, Ellen and Michael Dowling. *Presenting with Style: Advanced Strategies for Superior Presentations*. New York: Writer's Club Press, 2000.

Draves, William A. *How to Teach Adults*. Manhattan, KS: The Learning Resources Network, 1997.

Fine, Edith H., and Judith P. Josephson. *Nitty-Gritty Grammar, A Not-So-Serious Guide to Clear Communication*. Berkeley, CA: Ten Speed Press, 1998.

—————. *More Nitty-Gritty Grammar*. Berkeley, CA: Ten Speed Press, 2001.

Goleman, Daniel. *Emotional Intelligence*. New York: Bantam Books, 1995.

Griffith, Joe. *Speaker's Library of Business Stories, Anecdotes, and Humor*. Englewood Cliffs, NJ: Prentice Hall, 1990.

Heyman, Richard. *Why Didn't You Say That in the First Place?* San Francisco: Jossey-Bass, 1994.

Horn, Sam. *Tongue Fu.* New York: St. Martin's/Griffin, 1996.

Leech, Thomas. *Say It Like Shakespeare.* New York: McGraw-Hill, 2001.

Luft, Joseph. *Of Human Interaction.* Palo Alto, CA: National Press Books, 1969.

Lyerly, Barry, and Cyndi Maxey. *Training from the Heart.* Alexandria, VA: ASTD Press, 2000.

Maslow, Abraham H. *Motivation and Personality,* 2nd ed. New York: Harper and Row, 1970.

Mehrabian, Albert. *Silent Messages.* Belmont, CA: Wadsworth, 1981.

Orey, Maureen. *Successful Staffing in a Diverse Workplace.* Irving, CA: Richard Chang & Associates/Jossey-Bass/Pfeiffer, 1996.

Patterson, Kerry, Joseph Grenny, Ron McMillan, Al Switzler, and Stephen R. Covey. *Crucial Conversations: Tools for Talking When Stakes are High.* New York: McGraw-Hill, 2002.

Pease, Allan. *Body Language: How to Read Others' Thoughts by Their Gestures.* New South Wales, Australia: Camel Publishing Company, 1985.

Shister, Neil. *10 Minute Guide to Negotiating.* New York: Alpha Books, 1997.

Silberman, Mel, assisted by Carol Auerbach. *Active Training.* San Francisco: Jossey Bass/Pfeiffer, 1998.

Tipler, Julia. *Successful Negotiating.* New York: AMACOM, 2000.

Wilson, Joe B. *Mapping a Winning Training Approach.* Irving, CA: Richard Chang Associates Publishing, 1995.

Yankelovich, Daniel. *The Magic of Dialogue.* New York: Simon and Schuster, 2001.

◆

Maureen Orey has more than 20 years of experience in the fields of management, training, human resources, diversity, and career development. She holds a master's degree in education from the University of San Diego and a bachelor's degree in psychology from San Diego State University. Her first book is titled *Successful Staffing in a Diverse Workplace.*

As area manager for ASTD since 1997, Orey works with 45 chapters in 19 western states in the United States. She serves as a liaison between the local ASTD chapters and headquarters of the organization, providing strategic support and coaching to chapter leaders. She was recently twice awarded ASTD's 2004 Volunteer–Staff Partnership Award for her work with both the San Diego chapter and the National Advisors for Chapters. Orey, a past president of the San Diego chapter, is certified in servant leadership from the San Diego Leadership Institute, and has completed ASTD's Certificate in Human Performance Improvement. Orey stays active in her local community by participating with her children in karate, Girl Scouts, and Boy Scouts.

Jenni Prisk is an award-winning motivational speaker, communications coach. and trainer. In founding Prisk Communication in 1989, she set her mission to provide comprehensive and outstanding training in public speaking and communication skills so as to remove the associated risk and fear and to engender confidence, effectiveness, and positive results. She works with companies and individuals in diverse aspects of communication. A native of New Zealand, she holds a diploma in adult teaching and is qualified as a human relations and communications instructor for the New Zealand Marriage Guidance Council. She also has a diploma in speech and drama from London's Trinity College.

Following the September 11th terrorist attacks in 2001, Prisk founded Voices of Women (VOW), an international forum for peace-minded people, to foster global peace, justice, and equality around the world. For more information, visit www.voicesofwomen.org. Her diverse background includes working in the newspaper industry, where she received four writing awards. She received the *San Diego Business Journal*'s Award for Women Who Mean Business, was a finalist in Bank of America's first Enterprise Award Program, an honoree in the Women Together Awards, and a regional finalist in *Working Woman* magazine's first Entrepreneurial Excellence Award Program.

She is an associate member of TEC, an international community of chief executives, and a member of ASTD, the San Diego Press Club, the City Club of San Diego, and the Actors Alliance of San Diego. Prisk also serves on the San Diego Civic Solutions Committee and co-hosts "San Diego TheatreScene on Air" broadcast on World Talk Radio. She's an avid volunteer, giving time and energy to local charities, including Mama's Kitchen, the YWCA, the Old Globe Theatre, and the County Mental Health Center. She frequently anchors KPBS-TV San Diego fundraisers and writes a weekly column on what's happening in San Diego theatre for *TheatreScene* e-zine. She and her husband, Kim, live in the Sorrento Valley area of San Diego.